React 16 Essentials
Second Edition

A fast-paced, hands-on guide to designing and building scalable and maintainable web apps with React 16

Artemij Fedosejev

Adam Boduch

BIRMINGHAM - MUMBAI

React 16 Essentials
Second Edition

First published: August 2015

Second Edition: November 2017

Production reference: 2291117

Published by Packt Publishing Ltd.
Livery Place
35 Livery Street
Birmingham B3 2PB, UK.

ISBN 978-1-78712-604-6

www.packtpub.com

Credits

Authors
Artemij Fedosejev
Adam Boduch

Reviewers
Christopher Pitt
Konstantin Tarkus

Commissioning Editor
Ashwin Nair

Acquisition Editor
Dominic Shakeshaft

Project Editor
Radhika Atitkar

Content Development Editor
Radhika Atitkar

Technical Editor
Nidhisha Shetty

Copy Editor
Tom Jacob

Proofreader
Safis Editing

Indexer
Aishwarya Gangawane

Graphics
Jason Monteiro

Production Coordinator
Nilesh Mohite

Cover Work
Nilesh Mohite

About the Authors

Artemij Fedosejev is a technical lead living in London, United Kingdom. He is a self-taught web developer who has been a web developer since the early 2000s. Artemij earned his BSc in computer science from University College Cork, Ireland. He participated in the IGNITE Graduate Business Innovation Programme, where he built and launched a website that received the Most Innovative Project award. Artemij has played a key role in creating frontend architecture using React.js and Flux for various websites. Artemij created a number of open source projects, including Snapkite Engine, Snapkite Stream Client, and other projects.

Adam Boduch has been involved with large-scale JavaScript development for nearly 10 years. Before moving to frontend, he worked on several large-scale cloud computing products, using Python and Linux. No stranger to complexity, Adam has practical experience with real-world software systems and the scaling challenges they pose. Adam is the author of several JavaScript books, including *React and React Native* and *Mastering Immutable.js* by *Packt Publishing*. Adam is passionate about innovative user experiences and high performance.

About the Reviewers

Christopher Pitt is an author, speaker, and developer. He spends most of his time learning new technologies and teaching others about them. He has written about several topics, including JS game development, PHP framework usage, and how to create simple compilers.

Christopher has helped review the chapters on React 16 and Redux.

Konstantin Tarkus is a long-time software developer, and founder and CTO of Kriasoft—a software development company specializing in building web and cloud applications. He is the author of React Starter Kit—a popular open source boilerplate project for building isomorphic web applications with Node.js and React, which is used by many tech startups around the globe. You can reach out to him on Twitter: @koistya.

www.PacktPub.com

eBooks, discount offers, and more

Did you know that Packt offers eBook versions of every book published, with PDF and ePub files available? You can upgrade to the eBook version at `www.PacktPub.com` and as a print book customer, you are entitled to a discount on the eBook copy. Get in touch with us at `customercare@packtpub.com` for more details.

At `www.PacktPub.com`, you can also read a collection of free technical articles, sign up for a range of free newsletters and receive exclusive discounts and offers on Packt books and eBooks.

`https://www.packtpub.com/mapt`

Get the most in-demand software skills with Mapt. Mapt gives you full access to all Packt books and video courses, as well as industry-leading tools to help you plan your personal development and advance your career.

Why subscribe?

- Fully searchable across every book published by Packt
- Copy and paste, print, and bookmark content
- On demand and accessible via a web browser

Customer Feedback

Thanks for purchasing this Packt book. At Packt, quality is at the heart of our editorial process. To help us improve, please leave us an honest review on this book's Amazon page at https://www.amazon.com/dp/1787126048.

If you'd like to join our team of regular reviewers, you can email us at customerreviews@packtpub.com. We award our regular reviewers with free eBooks and videos in exchange for their valuable feedback. Help us be relentless in improving our products!

Table of Contents

Preface	**v**
Chapter 1: What's New in React 16	**1**
Rethinking rendering	**1**
The status quo	2
Running to completion	2
What are fibers?	4
Async and the road ahead	4
Better component error handling	5
Rendering multiple elements and strings	6
Rendering to portals	7
Summary	**8**
Chapter 2: Installing Powerful Tools for Your Project	**9**
Approaching our project	**11**
Installing Node.js and npm	**12**
Installing Git	**13**
Getting data from the Twitter Streaming API	**13**
Filtering data with Snapkite Engine	**14**
Creating the project structure	**17**
Creating package.json	**18**
Reusing Node.js modules	**19**
Building with Webpack	**20**
Creating a web page	**25**
Summary	**25**
Chapter 3: Creating Your First React Element	**27**
Understanding the virtual DOM	**28**
Installing React	**29**
Creating React elements with JavaScript	**30**
The type parameter	32

The props parameter	32
The children parameter	33
Rendering React elements	**38**
Creating React elements with JSX	**39**
Summary	**41**
Chapter 4: Creating Your First React Component	**43**
Stateless versus stateful	**43**
Creating your first stateless React component	**44**
Creating your first stateful React component	**50**
Summary	**55**
Chapter 5: Making Your React Components Reactive	**57**
Solving a problem using React	**57**
Planning your React application	**59**
Creating a container React component	**61**
Summary	**69**
Chapter 6: Using Your React Components with Another Library	**71**
Using another library in your React component	**71**
Understanding React component's lifecycle methods	**76**
Mounting methods	78
The componentWillMount method	78
The componentDidMount method	80
Unmounting methods	82
The componentWillUnmount method	83
Summary	**84**
Chapter 7: Updating Your React Components	**85**
Understanding component lifecycle updating methods	**85**
The componentWillReceiveProps method	86
The shouldComponentUpdate method	89
The componentWillUpdate method	89
The componentDidUpdate method	90
Setting default React component properties	**91**
Validating React component properties	**94**
Creating a Collection component	**97**
Summary	**103**
Chapter 8: Building Complex React Components	**105**
Creating the TweetList component	**105**
Creating the CollectionControls component	**110**
Creating the CollectionRenameForm component	**117**
Creating the Button component	**123**

Creating the CollectionExportForm component	125
Summary	126

Chapter 9: Testing Your React Application with Jest — **127**

Why write unit tests?	127
Creating test suites, specs, and expectations	128
Installing and running Jest	132
Creating multiple tests and expectations	134
Testing React components	140
Summary	152

Chapter 10: Supercharging Your React Architecture with Flux — **153**

Analyzing your web application's architecture	154
Understanding Flux	156
Creating a dispatcher	158
Creating an action creator	158
Creating a store	159
Summary	164

Chapter 11: Preparing Your React Application for Painless Maintenance with Flux — **165**

Decoupling concerns with Flux	166
Refactoring the Stream component	169
Creating CollectionStore	175
Creating CollectionActionCreators	180
Refactoring the Application component	182
Refactoring the Collection component	184
Refactoring the CollectionControls component	187
Refactoring the CollectionRenameForm component	189
Refactoring the TweetList component	192
Refactoring the StreamTweet component	193
Building and going beyond	194
Summary	194

Chapter 12: Refining Your Flux Apps with Redux — **195**

Why Redux?	195
One store to rule them all	195
Fewer moving parts	196
Uses the best parts of Flux	196
Controlling state with reducers	196
What are reducers?	196
Collection reducers	197
Adding tweets to collections	198
Removing tweets from collections	199

Setting the collection name	200
Editing collection names	200
Tweet reducers	**201**
Receiving tweets	201
Simplified action creators	201
Connecting components to an application state	**203**
Mapping state and action creators to props	203
Connecting the stream component	204
Connecting the StreamTweet component	205
Connecting the collection component	206
Connecting collection controls	208
Connecting the TweetList component	210
Creating stores and wiring your app	211
Summary	**213**
Index	**215**

Preface

A lot has changed in the React ecosystem since the first edition of React Essentials. More people are building React applications, there are mature libraries and frameworks that support React applications, and React 16 has been released. The explosive growth of React over such a short period of time can be attributed to a number of factors: the excellent community and related resources, the vastness of the React ecosystem and the maturation of certain staple projects, and of course, the React team and their willingness to make developer feedback a priority item as the project continues to evolve.

I feel privileged to be involved with such an important React title. As the name suggests, this book is aimed at teaching the essentials of React. This latest edition reflects changes in the latest version of React, using Redux for managing state, and the JavaScript language itself.

Join me. Let's become experts as React becomes the standard for building user interfaces.

What this book covers

Chapter 1, *What's New in React 16*, introduces the major changes in React 16. This includes the fundamental changes to how rendering and reconciliation work under the hood, and other new features that are exposed via the API.

Chapter 2, *Installing Powerful Tools for Your Project*, outlines the goal of this book and explains what modern tools you need to install in order to build React applications efficiently. It introduces each tool and provides step-by-step instructions on how to install each of them. Then, it creates a structure for the project that we'll be building in this book.

Chapter 3, *Creating Your First React Element*, explains how to install React and introduces virtual DOM. Then, it explains what React Element is and how to create and render one with native JavaScript syntax. Finally, it introduces the JSX syntax and shows how to create React Elements using JSX.

Chapter 4, *Creating Your First React Component*, introduces React components. It explains the difference between stateless and stateful React components and how to decide which one to use. Then, it guides you through the process of creating both kinds.

Chapter 5, *Making Your React Components Reactive*, explains how to solve a problem with React and walks you through the process of planning your React application. It creates a React component that encapsulates the entire React application that we build in this book. It explains the relationship between parent and child React components.

Chapter 6, *Using Your React Components with Another Library*, explores how to use third-party JavaScript libraries with your React components. It introduces the lifecycle of your React components, demonstrates how to use mounting methods, and shows how to create new React components for our book's project.

Chapter 7, *Updating Your React Components*, introduces the updating methods for the lifecycles of your React components. This covers how to use CSS styles in JavaScript. It explains how to validate and set the default properties of the components.

Chapter 8, *Building Complex React Components*, focuses on building more complex React components. It explores the details of how to implement different React components and how to put them together into one coherent and fully functional React application.

Chapter 9, *Testing Your React Application with Jest*, explains the idea of unit testing and how to write and run your unit tests with Jest. It also demonstrates how to test your React components. It discusses test suites, specs, expectations, and matchers.

Chapter 10, *Supercharging Your React Architecture with Flux*, discusses how to improve the architecture of our React application. It introduces the Flux architecture and explains the role of dispatchers, stores, and action creators.

Chapter 11, *Preparing Your React Application for Painless Maintenance with Flux*, explains how to decouple concerns in your React application with Flux. It refactors our React application to allow painless maintainability in the future.

Chapter 12, *Refining Your Flux Apps with Redux*, walks you through the main features of the Flux library, followed by a complete refactoring of an application to use Redux as the main mechanism to control state.

What you need for this book

First of all, you need the latest version of a modern web browser, such as Google Chrome or Mozilla Firefox:

- Google Chrome: `https://www.google.com/chrome/browser`
- Mozilla Firefox: `https://www.mozilla.org/en-US/firefox/new/`

Second, you will need to install Git, Node.js, and npm. You will find detailed instructions on how to install and use them in *Chapter 2, Installing Powerful Tools for Your Project*.

Finally, you will need a code editor. I recommend *Sublime Text* (`http://www.sublimetext.com`). Alternatively, you can use *Atom* (`https://atom.io`), *Brackets* (`http://brackets.io`), *Visual Studio Code* (`https://code.visualstudio.com`), or any other editor of your choice.

Who this book is for

This book is intended for frontend developers who want to build scalable and maintainable user interfaces for the web. Some core knowledge of JavaScript, HTML, and CSS is the only thing you need to know to start benefiting from the revolutionary ideas that React.js brings into the web development world. If you have previous experience with jQuery or Angular.js, then you will benefit from understanding how React.js is different and how to take advantage of integrating different libraries with it.

Conventions

In this book, you will find a number of styles of text that distinguish between different kinds of information. Here are some examples of these styles, and an explanation of their meaning.

Code words in text, database table names, folder names, filenames, file extensions, pathnames, dummy URLs, user input, and Twitter handles are shown as follows: Code words in text are shown as follows: "We can include other contexts through the use of the `include` directive."

A block of code is set as follows:

```
import React from 'react';
import { render } from 'react-dom';

const reactElement = React.createElement(
```

```
    'h1',
    { className: 'header' }
  );

  render(
    reactElement,
    document.getElementById('react-application')
  );
```

When we wish to draw your attention to a particular part of a code block, the relevant lines or items are set in bold:

```
<!doctype html>
  <html lang="en">
    <head>
      <title>Snapterest</title>
    </head>
    <body>
      <div id="react-application">
        I am about to learn the essentials of React.js.
      </div>
      <script src="./snapterest.js"></script>
    </body>
  </html>
```

Any command-line input or output is written as follows:

```
cd ~
git clone https://github.com/snapkite/snapkite-engine.git
```

New terms and **important words** are shown in bold. Words that you see on the screen, in menus or dialog boxes for example, appear in the text like this: "clicking on the **Next** button moves you to the next screen."

 Warnings or important notes appear in a box like this.

 Tips and tricks appear like this.

Reader feedback

Feedback from our readers is always welcome. Let us know what you think about this book—what you liked or may have disliked. Reader feedback is important for us to develop titles that you really get the most out of.

To send us general feedback, simply send an email to `feedback@packtpub.com`, and mention the book title via the subject of your message.

If there is a topic that you have expertise in and you are interested in either writing or contributing to a book, see our author guide on `www.packtpub.com/authors`.

Customer support

Now that you are the proud owner of a Packt book, we have a number of things to help you to get the most from your purchase.

Downloading the example code

You can download the example code files for all Packt books you have purchased from your account at `http://www.packtpub.com`. If you purchased this book elsewhere, you can visit `http://www.packtpub.com/support` and register to have the files emailed directly to you.

You can download the code files by following these steps:

1. Log in or register to our website using your email address and password.
2. Hover the mouse pointer on the **SUPPORT** tab at the top.
3. Click on **Code Downloads & Errata**.
4. Enter the name of the book in the **Search** box.
5. Select the book for which you're looking to download the code files.
6. Choose from the drop-down menu where you purchased this book from.
7. Click on **Code Download**.

You can also download the code files by clicking on the **Code Files** button on the book's webpage at the Packt Publishing website. This page can be accessed by entering the book's name in the **Search** box. Please note that you need to be logged in to your Packt account.

Once the file is downloaded, please make sure that you unzip or extract the folder using the latest version of:

- WinRAR / 7-Zip for Windows
- Zipeg / iZip / UnRarX for Mac
- 7-Zip / PeaZip for Linux

The code bundle for the book is also hosted on GitHub at `https://github.com/PacktPublishing/React-16-Essentials-Second-Edition`. We also have other code bundles from our rich catalog of books and videos available at `https://github.com/PacktPublishing/`. Check them out!

Downloading the color images of this book

We also provide you with a PDF file that has color images of the screenshots/diagrams used in this book. The color images will help you understand the changes in the output better. You can download this file from `https://www.packtpub.com/sites/default/files/downloads/React16EssentialsSecondEdition_ColorImages.pdf`.

Errata

Although we have taken every care to ensure the accuracy of our content, mistakes do happen. If you find a mistake in one of our books—maybe a mistake in the text or the code—we would be grateful if you would report this to us. By doing so, you can save other readers from frustration and help us improve subsequent versions of this book. If you find any errata, please report them by visiting `http://www.packtpub.com/submit-errata`, selecting your book, clicking on the **Errata Submission Form** link, and entering the details of your errata. Once your errata are verified, your submission will be accepted and the errata will be uploaded on our website, or added to any list of existing errata, under the Errata section of that title. Any existing errata can be viewed by selecting your title from `http://www.packtpub.com/support`.

Piracy

Piracy of copyright material on the internet is an ongoing problem across all media. At Packt, we take the protection of our copyright and licenses very seriously. If you come across any illegal copies of our works, in any form, on the Internet, please provide us with the location address or website name immediately so that we can pursue a remedy.

Please contact us at copyright@packtpub.com with a link to the suspected pirated material.

We appreciate your help in protecting our authors, and our ability to bring you valuable content.

Questions

You can contact us at questions@packtpub.com if you are having a problem with any aspect of the book, and we will do our best to address it.

1
What's New in React 16

The release of React 16 includes enough important changes to devote a chapter to them. This particular release took a comparatively long time to deliver. This is because the reconciliation internals—the part of React that figures out how to efficiently render component changes—was rewritten from the ground up. Compatibility was another factor: this rewrite has no major breaking API changes.

In this chapter, you'll learn about the major changes introduced in React 16:

- The major changes made to the reconciliation internals, and what they mean for React projects, going forward
- Confining errors to the sections of your application by setting error boundaries
- Creating components that render more than one element and components that render strings
- Rendering to portals

Rethinking rendering

You do not need a deep understanding of how the reconciliation internals of React work. This would defeat the purpose of React and how it encapsulates all of this work for us. However, understanding the motivation for the major internal changes that have happened in React 16, and how they work at a higher level, will help you think about how to best design your components today and for future React applications.

The status quo

React has established itself as one of the standards when it comes to choosing a library to help build user interfaces. The two key factors for this are its simplicity and its performance. React is simple because it has a small API surface that's easy to pick up and experiment with. React is performant because it minimizes the number of DOM operations it has to invoke by reconciling changes in a render tree.

There's an interplay between these two factors that has contributed to React's skyrocketing popularity. The good performance provided by React wouldn't be valuable if the API were difficult to use. The overarching value of React is that it's simple to use and performs well out of the box.

With the widespread adoption of React came the realization that its internal reconciliation mechanics could be improved. For example, some React applications update the component state faster than rendering can complete. Consider another example: changes to part of the render tree that aren't visible on the screen should have a lower priority than elements that the user can see. Issues like these are enough to degrade the user experience so that it doesn't feel as fluid as it could be.

How do you address these issues without disrupting the API and render tree reconciliation that work so well?

Running to completion

JavaScript is single-threaded and run-to-completion. This means that by default, any JavaScript code that you run will block any other browser tasks from running, such as painting the screen. This is why it's especially important that JavaScript code be fast. However, in some cases, even the performance of the React reconciliation code isn't enough to mask bottlenecks from the user. When presented with a new tree, React has no choice but to block the DOM updates and event listeners while it computes the new render tree.

One possible solution is to break the reconciliation work into smaller chunks, and arrange them in such a way that prevents the JavaScript run-to-completion thread from blocking important DOM updates. This would mean that the reconciler wouldn't have to render a complete tree, and then have to do it all over again because an event took place while the first render was taking place.

Let's look at a visual example of this problem:

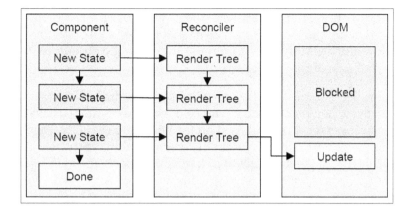

This figure demonstrates that any time state changes in a React component, nothing else can happen until rendering has completed. As you can see, reconciling entire trees can get expensive as the state changes pile up, and, all the while, the DOM is blocked from doing anything.

Reconciling the render tree is in lock-step with the run-to-completion semantics of JavaScript. In other words, React cannot pause what it's doing to let the DOM update. Let's now look at how React 16 is trying to change the preceding figure:

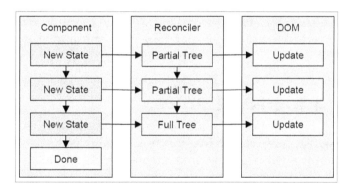

This version of the React render/reconciliation process looks similar to the previous version. In fact, nothing about the component on the left has changed – this is reflective of the unchanging API in React 16. There are some subtle but important differences though.

Let's start by looking at the reconciler. Instead of building a new render tree every time the component changes state, it renders a partial tree. Putting it another way, it performs a chunk of work that results in the creation of part of a render tree. The reason it doesn't complete the entire tree is so that the reconciliation process can pause and allow any DOM updates to run—you can see the difference in the DOM on the right-hand side of the image.

When the reconciler resumes building the render tree, it first checks to see if new state changes have taken place since it paused. If so, it takes the partially completed render tree and reuses what it can, based on the new state changes. Then, it keeps going until the next pause. Eventually, reconciliation completes. During reconciliation, the DOM has been given a chance to respond to events and to render any outstanding changes. Prior to React 16, this wasn't possible—you would have to wait until the entire tree was rendered before anything in the DOM could happen.

What are fibers?

In order to separate the job of rendering components into smaller units of work, React has created an abstraction called a **fiber**. A fiber represents a unit of rendering work that can be paused and resumed. It has other low-level properties such as priority and where the output of the fiber should be returned to when completed.

The code name of React 16 during development was React Fiber, because of this fundamental abstraction that enables scheduling pieces of the overall rendering work to provide a better user experience. React 16 marks the initial release of this new reconciliation architecture, but it's not done yet. For example, everything is still synchronous.

Async and the road ahead

React 16 lays the groundwork for the ultimate goal of asynchronous rendering in the next major release. The main reason that this functionality isn't included in React 16 is because the team wanted to get the fundamental reconciliation changes out into the wild. There are a few other new features that needed to be released too, which we'll go over in the following sections.

Once asynchronous rendering capabilities are introduced into React, you shouldn't have to modify any code. Instead, you might notice improved performance in certain areas of your application that would benefit from prioritized and scheduled rendering.

Better component error handling

React 16 introduces better error-handling capabilities for components. The concept is called an **error boundary**, and it's implemented as a lifecycle method that is called when any child components throw an exception. The parent class that implements `componentDidCatch()` is the error boundary. You could have different boundaries throughout your application, depending on how your features are organized.

The motivation for this functionality is to give the application an opportunity to recover from certain errors. Prior to React 16, if a component threw an error, the entire app would stop. This might not be ideal, especially if an issue with a minor component stops critical components from working.

Let's create an `App` component with an error boundary:

```
class App extends Component {
  state = {}

  componentDidCatch(err) {
    this.setState({ err: err.message });
  }

  render() {
    return (<p><MyError err={this.state.err}/></p>);
  }
}
```

The `App` component does nothing but render `MyError` — a component that intentionally throws an error. When this happens, the `componentDidCatch()` method is called with the error as an argument. You can then use this value to change the state of the component. In this example, it sets the error message in the `err` state. Then, `App` will attempt to re-render.

As you can see, `this.state.err` is passed to `MyError` as a property. During the first render, this value is undefined. When `App` catches the error thrown by `MyError`, the error is passed back to the component. Let's look at `MyError` now:

```
const MyError = (props) => {
  if (props.err) {
    return <b style={{color: 'red'}}>{props.err}</b>;
  }

  throw new Error('epic fail');
};
```

This component throws an error with the message `'epic fail'`. When `App` catches this error, it renders `MyError` with an `err` prop. When this happens, it simply renders the error string in red. This just happens to be the strategy I've chosen for this app; always check for an error state before invoking the errant behavior again. In `MyError`, the application as a whole is recovered by not executing `throw new Error('epic fail')` for a second time.

With `componentDidCatch()`, you're free; set any strategy you like for error recovery. Usually, you can't recover a specific component that fails.

Rendering multiple elements and strings

Since React was first released, the rule was that components could only render one element. This has changed in two important ways in React 16. First, you can now return a collection of elements from your component. This simplifies cases where rendering sibling elements would drastically simplify things. Second, you can now render plain text content.

Both of these changes result in fewer elements on the page. By allowing sibling elements to be rendered by components, you don't have to wrap them with an element for the sake of returning a single element. By rendering strings, you can render test content as the child or another component, without having to wrap it in an element.

Here's what rendering multiple elements looks like:

```
const Multi = () => [
  'first sibling',
  'second sibling'
].map((v, i) => <p key={i}>{v}</p>);
```

Note that you have to provide a `key` property for elements in a collection. Now let's add an element that returns a string value:

```
const Label = () => 'Name:';

const MultiWithString = () => [
  'first sibling',
  'second sibling'
].map((v, i) => <p key={i}><Label/> {v}</p>);
```

The `Label` component simply returns a string as its rendered content. The `p` element renders `Label` as a child, adjacent to the `{v}` value. When components can return strings, you have more options for composing the elements that make up your UI.

Rendering to portals

The final new feature of React 16 that I want to introduce is the notion of portals. Normally, the rendered output of a component is placed where the JSX element is located within the tree. However, there are times when we have greater control over where the rendered output of our components ends up. For example, what if you wanted to render a component outside of the root React element?

Portals allow components to specify their container element at render time. Imagine that you want to display notifications in your application. Several components at different locations on the screen need the ability to render notifications at one specific spot on the screen. Let's take a look at how you can target elements using portals:

```
import React, { Component } from 'react';
import { createPortal } from 'react-dom';
class MyPortal extends Component {
  constructor(...args) {
    super(...args);
    this.el = document.createElement('strong');
  }

  componentWillMount() {
    document.body.appendChild(this.el);
  }

  componentWillUnmount() {
    document.body.removeChild(this.el);
  }

  render() {
    return createPortal(
      this.props.children,
      this.el
    );
  }
};
```

In the constructor of this component, the target element is created and stored in the el property. Then, in componentWillMount(), the element is appended to the document body. You don't actually need to create the target element in your component—you can use an existing element instead. The componentWillUnmount() method removes this element.

In the `render()` method, the `createPortal()` function is used to create the portal. It takes two arguments — the content to render and the target DOM element. In this case, it's passing its child properties. Let's take a look at how `MyPortal` is used:

```
class App extends Component {
  render() {
    return (
      <div>
        <p>Main content</p>
        <MyPortal>Bro, you just notified me!</MyPortal>
      </div>
    );
  }
}
```

The end result is that the text that's passed to `MyPortal` is rendered as a strong element outside of the root React element. Before portals, you would have to resort to some kind of imperative workaround in order for something like this to work. Now, we can just render the notification in the same context that it's needed in — it just happens to be inserted somewhere else in the DOM in order to display correctly.

Summary

The goal of this chapter was to introduce you to the substantial changes in React 16. Remarkably, there are almost no compatibility issues with the prior React release. This is because most of the changes were internal and didn't require changes in the API. A couple of new features were added as well.

The headline of React 16 is its new reconciliation internals. Rather than trying to reconcile everything any time a component changes state, the reconciliation work is now broken into smaller units. These units can be prioritized, scheduled, paused, and resumed. In the near future, React will take full advantage of this new architecture and start rendering units of work asynchronously.

You also learned how to use the new error boundary functionality in React components. Using error boundaries allows you to recover from component errors without taking down the entire application. Then, you learned that React components can now return collections of components. This is just like when you render a collection of components. Now you can do this directly from components. Finally, you learned how to render components to nonstandard locations using portals.

In the next chapter, you'll learn how to build reactive components.

2
Installing Powerful Tools for Your Project

Here is a great quote by Charles F. Kettering:

"My interest is in the future because I am going to spend the rest of my life there."

This brilliant inventor has left software engineers with the single most important piece of advice way before we even started thinking how to write software. Yet, half a century later, we're still figuring out why we end up with spaghetti code or the "spaghetti mental model."

Have you ever been in a situation where you inherit code from a previous developer and spend weeks trying to understand how everything works because no blueprints were made available, and the pseudo-self-explanatory-code became too hard to debug? Better yet, the project keeps growing and so does its complexity. Making or breaking changes is dangerous and no one wants to touch that "ugly" legacy code. Rewriting the whole codebase is way too expensive, so the current one is supported by introducing new bug fixes and patches every day. The cost of maintaining software is way higher than the original cost of developing it.

What does it mean to write software for the future today? I think it boils down to creating a simple mental model that doesn't change, no matter how big your project becomes over time. When the size of your project grows, the complexity always stays the same. This mental model is your blueprint, and once you understand it, you will understand how your software works.

If you take a look at the modern web development, and in particular, the frontend development, you'll notice that we live in exciting times. Internet companies and individual developers are tackling problems of speed and cost of development versus code and user experience quality.

In 2013, Facebook released React—an open source JavaScript library for building user interfaces. You can read more about it at `http://facebook.github.io/react/`. In early 2015, Tom Occhino from Facebook has summarized what makes React so powerful:

> *"React wraps an imperative API with a declarative one. React's real power lies in how it makes you to write code."*

Declarative programming results in less code. It tells a computer what to do without specifying how, while an imperative style of programming describes how to do it. JavaScript calling the DOM API is an example of imperative programming. jQuery is another such example.

Facebook has been using React in production for years along with Instagram and other companies. It works for small projects too; here is an example of a shopping list built with React: `http://fedosejev.github.io/shopping-list-react`. I think React is one of the best JavaScript libraries used for building user interfaces that is available for developers today.

My goal is that you understand the fundamental principles of React. To achieve this, I will introduce you to one React concept at a time, explain it, and show how you can apply it. Step by step we'll build a real-time web application, raise important questions along the way, and discuss solutions that React provides us with.

You will learn about Flux/Redux and the unidirectional flow of data. Together with Flux/Redux and React, we'll create a predictable and manageable code base that you will be able to expand by adding new features, without scaling its complexity. The mental model of how your web application works will stay the same no matter how many new features you add later on.

As with any new technology, there are things that work very differently from the way that you're used to. React is no exception. In fact, some of the core concepts of React might look counter-intuitive, thought provoking, or even like a step backward. Don't rush to any conclusions. As you would expect, a lot of thought went into how React works, from experienced Facebook engineers who build and use React in production in business-critical applications. My advice to you is to keep your mind open while learning React, and I believe that at the end of this book, these new concepts will settle in and make great sense to you.

Join me in this journey of learning React and following Charles F. Kettering's advice. Let's take care of our future!

Approaching our project

I firmly believe that the best motivation for learning new technology is a project that excites you that you can't wait to build. As an experienced developer, you've probably already built a number of successful commercial projects that share certain product features, design patterns, and even target audiences. In this book, I want you to build a project that feels like a breath of fresh air. A project, which you most likely wouldn't build in your day-to-day work. It has to be a fun endeavor, which will not only educate you but also satisfy your curiosity and stretch your imagination. However, assuming that you're a busy professional, this project shouldn't be a time-consuming, long-term commitment for you either.

Enter **Snapterest**—a web application that allows you to discover and collect public photos posted on Twitter. Think of it as a Pinterest (`www.pinterest.com`) with the only source of pictures being Twitter. We will implement a fully functional website with the following core functionalities:

- Receiving and displaying tweets in real time
- Adding and removing tweets to/from a collection
- Reviewing collected tweets
- Exporting a collection of tweets as an HTML snippet that you can share

When you start working on a new project, the very first thing that you do is to get your tools ready. For this project, we will be using a number of tools that you might not be familiar with, so let's discuss what they are, and how you can install and configure them.

If you have any trouble with installing and configuring tools and modules from this chapter, then go to `https://github.com/PacktPublishing/React-Essentials-Second-Edition` and create a new issue; describe what you're doing and what error message you're getting. I believe our community will help you to resolve your issue.

In this book, I'll assume that you're working on a Macintosh or Windows computer. If you're a Unix user, then most likely you would know your package manager very well, and it should be easy enough for you to install the tools that you will learn about in this chapter.

Let's start with the installation of Node.js.

Installing Node.js and npm

Node.js is a platform that allows us to write server-side applications with a client-side language that we're all familiar with — JavaScript. However, the real benefit of Node.js is that it uses an event-driven, nonblocking I/O model, which is perfect for building data-intensive, real-time applications. It means that with Node.js, we should be able to handle an incoming stream of tweets and process them as soon as they arrive; just what we need for our project.

Let's install Node.js. We'll be using version 8.7.0 because at the time of writing this book, that's the latest version of Node.js. Jest is a testing framework from Facebook that you'll learn about in *Chapter 9, Testing Your React Application with Jest*.

Download the installation package for your OS from one of these links:

- OS X: http://nodejs.org/dist/v8.7.0/node-v8.7.0.pkg
- Windows 64-bit: http://nodejs.org/dist/v8.7.0/node-v8.7.0-x64.msi
- Windows 32-bit: http://nodejs.org/dist/v8.7.0/node-v8.7.0-x86.msi

Run the downloaded package and follow the installation steps that Node.js will prompt you with. Once finished, check whether you have successfully installed Node.js. Open Terminal/Command Prompt, and type the following command:

```
node -v
```

The output is as follows (don't worry if your version doesn't match exactly):

```
V8.7.0
```

Node.js has a very rich ecosystem of modules that is available for us to use. A module is a Node.js application that you can reuse in your own Node.js application. At the time of writing, there are over 500,000 modules. How do you manage such a wide diversity of Node.js modules? Meet **npm**, a package manager that manages Node.js modules. In fact, npm is shipped together with Node.js, so you've got it installed already. Type the following in Terminal/Command Prompt:

```
npm -v
```

You should see the following output (don't worry if your version doesn't match exactly):

```
5.5.1
```

You can learn more about npm at www.npmjs.com. Now we are ready to start with the installation of Node.js applications.

Installing Git

In this book, we'll be using Git to install Node.js modules. If you haven't installed Git yet, visit `https://git-scm.com/book/en/v2/Getting-Started-Installing-Git` and follow the installation instructions for your OS.

Getting data from the Twitter Streaming API

The data for our React application will come from Twitter. Twitter has a **Streaming API** that anyone can plug into and start receiving an endless flow of public tweets in the JSON format.

To start using the Twitter Streaming API, you'll need to perform the following steps:

1. Create a Twitter account. For this, go to `https://twitter.com` and sign up; or sign in if you already have an account.

2. Create a new Twitter app by navigating to `https://apps.twitter.com`, and click on **Create New App**. You will need to fill the **Application Details** form, agree with **Developer Agreement**, and click on **Create your Twitter application**. Now you should see your application's page. Switch to the **Keys and Access Tokens** tab.

In the **Application Settings** section of this page, you'll find two vital pieces of information:

- **Consumer Key (API Key)**, for example, `jqRDrAlKQCbCbu2o4iclpnvem`
- **Consumer Secret (API Secret)**, for example, `wJcdogJih7uLpjzcs2JtAvdSyCVlqHIRUWI70aHOAf7E3wWIgD`

Take a note of these; we will need them later in this chapter.

Now we need to generate an access token. On the same page, you'll see the **Your Access Token** section that is empty. Click on the **Create my access token** button. It creates two pieces of information:

- **Access Token**, for example, `12736172-R017ah2pE2OCtmi46IAE2n0z3u2DV6IqsEcPa0THR`
- **Access Token Secret**, for example, `4RTJJWIezIDcs5VX1PMVZolXGZG7L3Ez7Iz1gMdZucDaM`

Take a note of these too. An access token is unique to you and you should not share it with anyone. Keep it private.

Now we have everything that we need to start using Twitter's Streaming API.

Filtering data with Snapkite Engine

The amount of tweets that you'll receive via the Twitter Streaming API is more than you can ever consume, so we need to find a way to filter that stream of data into a meaningful set of tweets that we can display and interact with. I recommend that you take a quick look at the Twitter Streaming API documentation at `https://dev.twitter.com/streaming/overview`, and in particular, take a look at this page that describes the way you can filter an incoming stream at `https://dev.twitter.com/streaming/reference/post/statuses/filter`. You'll notice that Twitter provides very few filters that we can apply, so we need to find a way to filter that stream of data even further.

Luckily, there is a Node.js application just for this. It's called **Snapkite Engine**. It connects to the Twitter Streaming API, filters it using the available filters and according to the rules that you define, and outputs the filtered tweets to a web socket connection. Our proposed React application can listen to the events on that socket connection and process tweets as they arrive.

Let's install Snapkite Engine. First, you need to clone the Snapkite Engine repository. Cloning means that you're copying the source code from a GitHub server to your local directory. In this book, I'll assume that your local directory is your home directory. Open Terminal/Command Prompt and type the following commands:

```
cd ~
git clone https://github.com/snapkite/snapkite-engine.git
```

This should create the `~/snapkite-engine/` folder. We're now going to install all the other node modules that `snapkite-engine` depends on. One of them is the `node-gyp` module. Depending on what platform you're using, Unix or Windows, you will need to install other tools that are listed on this web page: `https://github.com/TooTallNate/node-gyp#installation`.

Once you install them, you're ready to install the `node-gyp` module:

```
npm install -g node-gyp
```

Now navigate to the `~/snapkite-engine` directory:

```
cd snapkite-engine/
```

Then run the following command:

```
npm install
```

This command will install the Node.js modules that Snapkite Engine depends on. Now let's configure Snapkite Engine. Assuming that you're in the `~/snapkite-engine/` directory, copy the `./example.config.json` file to `./config.json` by running the following command:

```
cp example.config.json config.json
```

Alternatively, if you're using Windows, run this command:

```
copy example.config.json config.json
```

Open `config.json` in your favorite text editor. We will now edit the configuration properties. Let's start with `trackKeywords`. This is where we will tell what keywords we want to track. If we want to track the `"my"` keyword, then set it as follows:

```
"trackKeywords": "my"
```

Next, we need to set our Twitter Streaming API keys. Set `consumerKey`, `consumerSecret`, `accessTokenKey`, and `accessTokenSecret` to the keys you saved when you created your Twitter App. Other properties can be set to their defaults. If you're curious to learn about what they are, check out the Snapkite Engine documentation at `https://github.com/snapkite/snapkite-engine`.

Our next step is to install Snapkite Filters. **Snapkite Filter** is a Node.js module that validates tweets according to a set of rules. There are a number of Snapkite Filters out there, and we can use any combination of them to filter our stream of tweets as we like. You can find a list of all the available Snapkite Filters at `https://github.com/snapkite/snapkite-filters`.

In our application, we'll use the following Snapkite Filters:

- **Is Possibly Sensitive**: `https://github.com/snapkite/snapkite-filter-is-possibly-sensitive`
- **Has Mobile Photo**: `https://github.com/snapkite/snapkite-filter-has-mobile-photo`
- **Is Retweet**: `https://github.com/snapkite/snapkite-filter-is-retweet`
- **Has Text**: `https://github.com/snapkite/snapkite-filter-has-text`

Let's install them. Navigate to the ~/snapkite-engine/filters/ directory:

```
cd ~/snapkite-engine/filters/
```

Then clone all Snapkite Filters by running these commands:

```
git clone https://github.com/snapkite/snapkite-filter-is-possibly-sensitive.git
```

```
git clone https://github.com/snapkite/snapkite-filter-has-mobile-photo.git
```

```
git clone https://github.com/snapkite/snapkite-filter-is-retweet.git
```

```
git clone https://github.com/snapkite/snapkite-filter-has-text.git
```

The next step is to configure them. In order to do so, you need to create a configuration file for each Snapkite Filter in a **JSON** format and define some properties in it. Luckily, each Snapkite Filter comes with an example configuration file that we can duplicate and edit as needed. Assuming that you're in the ~/snapkite-engine/filters/ directory, run the following commands (use copy and replace the forward slashes with backward slashes on Windows):

```
cp snapkite-filter-is-possibly-sensitive/example.config.json snapkite-filter-is-possibly-sensitive/config.json
```

```
cp snapkite-filter-has-mobile-photo/example.config.json snapkite-filter-has-mobile-photo/config.json
```

```
cp snapkite-filter-is-retweet/example.config.json snapkite-filter-is-retweet/config.json
```

```
cp snapkite-filter-has-text/example.config.json snapkite-filter-has-text/config.json
```

We don't need to change any of the default settings in these config.json files, as they're already configured to fit our purposes.

Finally, we need to tell Snapkite Engine which Snapkite Filters it should use. Open the ~/snapkite-engine/config.json file in a text editor and look for this:

```
    "filters": []
```

Now replace that with the following:

```
    "filters": [
      "snapkite-filter-is-possibly-sensitive",
      "snapkite-filter-has-mobile-photo",
      "snapkite-filter-is-retweet",
      "snapkite-filter-has-text"
    ]
```

Well done! You've successfully installed Snapkite Engine with a number of Snapkite Filters. Now let's check if we can run it. Navigate to `~/snapkite-engine/` and run the following command:

```
npm start
```

You should see no error messages, but if you do and you're not sure how to fix them, then go to `https://github.com/fedosejev/react-essentials/issues`, create a new issue, and copy and paste the error message that you get.

Next, let's set up our project's structure.

Creating the project structure

Now it's time to create our project structure. Organizing source files may sound like a simple task, but a well-thought-out project structure organization helps us understand the underlying architecture of our application. You'll see an example of this later in this book, when we'll talk about the Flux application architecture. Let's start by creating our root project directory named `snapterest` inside your home directory `~/snapterest/`.

Then, inside it, we will create two other directories:

- `~/snapterest/source/`: Here, we'll store our source JavaScript files
- `~/snapterest/build/`: Here, we'll put compiled JavaScript files and an HTML file

Now, inside `~/snapterest/source/`, create the `components/` folder so that your project structure would look like this:

- `~/snapterest/source/components/`
- `~/snapterest/build/`

Now when we have our fundamental project structure ready, let's start populating it with our application files. First, we need to create our main application file `app.js` in the `~/snapterest/source/` directory. This file will be the entry point to our application, `~/snapterest/source/app.js`.

Leave it empty for now, as we have a more pressing matter to discuss.

Creating package.json

Have you ever heard of **D.R.Y.** before? It stands for **Don't Repeat Yourself**, and it promotes one of the core principles in software development—code reuse. The best code is the code that you don't need to write. In fact, one of our goals in this project is to write as little code as possible. You might not realize this yet, but React helps us achieve this goal. Not only it saves us time, but if we also decide to maintain and improve our project in the future, it will save us even more time in the long run.

When it comes to not writing our code, we can apply the following strategies:

* Writing our code in a declarative programming style
* Reusing code written by someone else

In this project, we'll be using both techniques. The first one is covered by React itself. React leaves us no choice but to write our JavaScript code in a declarative style. This means that instead of telling our web browser how to do what we want (like we do with jQuery), we just tell it what we want it to do, and the how part is explained by React. That's a win for us.

Node.js and npm cover the second technique. I mentioned earlier in this chapter that there are hundreds of thousands of different Node.js applications available for us to use. This means that most likely someone already implemented the functionality that our application depends on.

The question is, where do you get all these Node.js applications that we want to reuse? We can install them via the `npm install <package-name>` command. In the npm context, a Node.js application is called a **package**, and each **npm package** has a `package.json` file that describes the metadata associated with that package. You can learn more about the fields that are stored in `package.json` at `https://docs.npmjs.com/files/package.json`.

Before we install our dependency packages, we will initialize a package for our own project. Normally, `package.json` is only required when you want to submit your package to the npm registry so that others can reuse your Node.js application. We're not going to build a Node.js application, and we're not going to submit our project to npm. Remember that `package.json` is technically only a metadata file that the `npm` command understands, and as such, we can use it to store a list of dependencies that our application requires. Once we store a list of dependencies in `package.json`, we can easily install them anytime with the `npm install` command; npm will figure out from where to get them automatically.

How do we create the `package.json` file for our own application? Luckily, npm comes with an interactive tool that asks us a bunch of questions and then based on our answers, creates `package.json` for our project.

Make sure that you're located in the `~/snapterest/` directory. In Terminal/ Command Prompt, run the following command:

```
npm init
```

The first thing it will ask you is your package name. It will suggest a default name, the name of the directory you're located in. It should suggest `name: (snapterest)` in our case. Press *Enter* to accept the proposed default name (`snapterest`). The next question is the version of your package, that is, `version: (1.0.0)`. Press *Enter*. These two would be the most important fields if we were planning to submit our package to npm for others to reuse. Because we're not going to submit it to npm, we can confidently accept defaults for all the questions that we were asked. Keep pressing *Enter* until `npm init` completes its execution and exits. Then, if you go to your `~/snapterest/` directory, you will find a new file there—`package.json`.

Now we're ready to install other Node.js applications that we're going to reuse. An application that is built of multiple individual applications is called **modular**, whereas individual applications are called **modules**. This is what we'll call our Node.js dependencies from now on—Node.js modules.

Reusing Node.js modules

As I mentioned earlier, there will be a step in our development process called **building**. During this step, our build script will take our source files and all our Node.js dependency packages and transform them into a single file that web browsers can successfully execute. The most important part of this building process is called **packaging**. But what do we need to package and why? Let's think about it. I briefly mentioned earlier that we're not creating a Node.js application, but yet we're talking about reusing Node.js modules. Does this mean that we'll be reusing Node.js modules in a nonNode.js application? Is that even possible? It turns out that there is a way of doing this.

Webpack is a tool used for bundling all your dependency files together in such a way that you can reuse Node.js modules in client-side JavaScript applications. You can learn more about Webpack at `http://webpack.js.org`. To install Webpack, run the following command from inside the `~/snapterest/` directory:

```
npm install --save-dev webpack
```

Notice the `--save-dev` flag. It tells npm to add Webpack to our `package.json` file as a development dependency. Adding a module name to our `package.json` file as a dependency allows us to record what dependencies we're using, and we can easily install them later with the `npm install` command, if needed. There is a distinction between the dependencies that are required to run your application and the ones that are required to develop your application. Webpack is used at build time, and not at runtime, so it's a development dependency. Hence, the use of the `--save-dev` flag. If you check the content of your `package.json` file now, you'll see this (don't worry if your Webpack version doesn't match exactly):

```
"devDependencies": {
    "webpack": "^2.2.1"
}
```

Notice that npm created a new folder in your `~/snapterest/` directory called `node_modules`. This is the place where it puts all your local dependency modules.

Congrats on installing your first Node.js module! Webpack will allow us to use Node.js modules in our client-side JavaScript applications. It will be a part of our build process. Now let's take a closer look at our build process.

Building with Webpack

Today, any modern client-side application represents a mix of many concerns that are addressed individually by various technologies. Addressing each concern individually simplifies the overall process of managing the project's complexity. The downside of this approach is that at some point in your project, you need to put together all the individual parts into one coherent application. Just like the robots in an automotive factory that assemble cars from individual parts, developers have something called as build-tools that assemble their projects from individual modules. This process is called the **build** process, and depending on the size and complexity of your project, it can take anywhere from milliseconds to hours to build.

Webpack will help us to automate our build process. First, we need to configure Webpack. Assuming you're in your `~/snapterest/` directory, create a new `webpack.config.js` file.

Now let's describe our build process in the `webpack.config.js` file. In this file, we'll create a JavaScript object that describes how to bundle our source files. We want to export that configuration object as a Node.js module. Yes, we'll treat our `webpack.config.js` file as a Node.js module. To do this, we'll assign our empty configuration object to a special `module.exports` property:

```
const path = require('path');
module.exports = {};
```

The `module.exports` property is a part of the Node.js API. It's a way of telling Node.js that whenever someone imports our module they will get access to that object. So what should this object look like? This is where I recommend that you to take a look at Webpack's documentation and read about the core concepts of Webpack, from the following link: `https://webpack.js.org/concepts/`

The first property of our configuration object will be the `entry` property:

```
module.exports = {
  entry: './source/app.js',
};
```

As the name suggests, the `entry` property describes the entry point to our web application. In our case, the value for this property is `./source/app.js` — this is the first file that starts our application.

The second property of our configuration object will be the `output` property:

```
output: {
  path: path.resolve(__dirname, 'build'),
  filename: 'snapterest.js'
},
```

The `output` property tells Webpack where to output the resulting bundle file. In our case, we're saying that we want the resulting bundle file to be called `snapterest.js` and it should be saved to the `./build` directory.

Webpack treats every source file as a module, which means all our JavaScript source files will be treated as modules that Webpack will need to bundle together. How do we explain this to Webpack?

We do this with the help of the third property of our configuration object called `module`:

```
module: {
  rules: [
    {
      test: /\.js$/,
      use: [
        {
          loader: 'babel-loader',
          options: {
            presets: ['react', 'latest'],
            plugins: ['transform-class-properties']
          }
        }
```

```
        ],
        exclude: path.resolve(__dirname, 'node_modules')
      }
    ]
  }
```

As you can see, our `module` property gets an object as its value. This object has a single property called `rules` — an array of rules where each rule describes how to create Webpack modules from different source files. Let's take a closer look at our rules.

We have a single rule that tells Webpack how to handle our source JavaScript files:

```
{
  test: /\.js$/,
  use: [
    {
      loader: 'babel-loader',
      options: {
        presets: ['react', 'latest'],
        plugins: ['transform-class-properties']
      }
    }
  ],
  exclude: path.resolve(__dirname, 'node_modules')
}
```

This rule has three properties: `test`, `use`, and `exclude`. The `test` property tells Webpack which files this rule applies to. It does this by matching our source file names against the RegEx expression that we specified as a value for our `test` property: `/\.js$/`. If you're familiar with RegEx, then you'll recognise that `/\.js$/` will match all filenames that end with `.js`. This is exactly what we want: to bundle all our JavaScript files.

When Webpack finds and loads all source JavaScript files, it tries to interpret them as plain JavaScript files. However, our JavaScript files won't be plain JavaScript files, instead they will have ECMAScript 2016 syntax, as well as React-specific syntax.

How can Webpack understand all that nonplain JavaScript syntax? With the help of Webpack loaders we can transform nonplain JavaScript syntax in to plain JavaScript. A Webpack loader is a transformation applied to a source file. Our `use` property describes a list of transformations that we want to apply:

```
use: [
  {
    loader: 'babel-loader',
    options: {
```

```
        presets: ['react', 'latest'],
        plugins: ['transform-class-properties']
      }
    }
  ],
```

We have one transformation that is responsible for transforming our React-specific syntax and ECMAScript 2016 syntax into plain JavaScript:

```
{
  loader: 'babel-loader',
  options: {
    presets: ['react', 'latest'],
    plugins: ['transform-class-properties']
  }
}
```

Webpack transformations are described with objects that have the `loader` and `options` properties. The `loader` property tells Webpack which loader performs the transformation, and the `options` property tells it which options should be passed to that loader. The loader that will transform our ECMAScript 2016 and React-specific syntaxes in to plain JavaScript is called `babel-loader`. This specific transformation process is called **transpilation** or **source-to-source compilation** — it takes source code written in one syntax and transforms it into a source code written in another syntax. We're using one of the most popular JavaScript transpilers today, called **Babel**: `https://babeljs.io`. Webpack has a Babel loader that uses Babel transpiler to transform our source code. Babel loader comes as a separate Node.js module. Let's install this module and add it to the list of our development dependencies. Assuming you're in your `~/snapterest/` directory, run this command:

npm install babel-core babel-loader --save-dev

The `options` property of our Webpack loader has a couple of Babel presents: `latest` and `react` and a Babel `transform-class-properties` plugin:

```
options: {
  presets: ['react', 'latest'],
  plugins: ['transform-class-properties']
}
```

These are Babel plugins that transpile different syntaxes: the `latest` plugin transpiles the syntaxes of ECMAScript 2015, ECMAScript 2016, and ECMAScript 2017 to old JavaScript syntax, and the `react` plugin transpiles React-specific syntax to plain JavaScript syntax, while the `transform-class-properties` plugin transpiles class properties.

These Babel plugins are distributed as standalone Node.js modules, which we need to install separately. Assuming you're in your `~/snapterest/` directory, run the following command:

```
npm install babel-preset-latest babel-preset-react babel-plugin-
transform-class-properties --save-dev
```

Finally, we have the third property in our Webpack rule called `exclude`:

```
exclude: path.resolve(__dirname, 'node_modules')
```

This property tells Webpack to exclude the `node_modules` directory from our transformation process.

Now we have our `webpack.config.js` file ready. Before we run our bundling process for the first time, let's add a new script called `start` to our `package.json` file:

```
"scripts": {
  "start": "webpack -p --config webpack.config.js",
  "test": "echo \"Error: no test specified\" && exit 1"
},
```

Now if you run `npm run start` or `npm start`, npm will run the `webpack -p --config webpack.config.js` command. This command runs Webpack that bundles our source files for production using the `webpack.config.js` file.

We're ready to bundle our source files! Navigate to your `~/snapterest/` directory and run this command:

```
npm start
```

In the output, you should see the following:

```
Version: webpack 2.2.1
Time: 1151ms
 Asset        Size  Chunks             Chunk Names
app.js  519 bytes       0  [emitted]  main
   [0] ./source/app.js 24 bytes {0} [built]
```

More importantly, if you check your project's `~/snapterest/build/` directory, you'll notice that it now has the `snapterest.js` file with some code already inside of it—that's our (empty) JavaScript application with some Node.js modules that are ready to run in a web browser!

Creating a web page

If you're hungry for some React goodness, then I have great news for you! We're almost there. All that's left to do is to create `index.html` with a link to our `snapterest.js` script.

Create the `index.html` file in the `~/snapterest/build/` directory. Add the following HTML markup to it:

```html
<!doctype html>
<html lang="en">
  <head>
    <meta charset="utf-8" />
    <meta http-equiv="x-ua-compatible" content="ie=edge, chrome=1" />
    <title>Snapterest</title>
    <link rel="stylesheet" href="https://maxcdn.bootstrapcdn.com/
    bootstrap/3.3.7/css/bootstrap.min.css">
  </head>
  <body>
    <div id="react-application">
      I am about to learn the essentials of React.js.
    </div>
    <script src="./snapterest.js"></script>
  </body>
</html>
```

Open `~/snapterest/build/index.html` in a web browser. You should see the following text: **I am about to learn the essentials of React.js**. That's right, we have finished setting up our project, and it's time to get to know React!

Summary

In this chapter, you learned why we should use React to build user interfaces for modern web applications. Then, we discussed the project that we'll be building in this book. Finally, we installed all the right tools and created the project's structure.

In the next chapter, we'll install React, take a closer look at how React works, and create our first React Element.

3

Creating Your First
React Element

Creating a simple web application today involves writing HTML, CSS, and JavaScript code. The reason we use three different technologies is that we want to separate three different concerns:

- Content (HTML)
- Styling (CSS)
- Logic (JavaScript)

This separation works great for creating a web page because traditionally, we had different people working on different parts of our web page: one person structured the content using HTML and styled it using CSS, and then another person implemented the dynamic behavior of various elements on that web page using JavaScript. It was a content-centric approach.

Today, we mostly don't think of a website as a collection of web pages anymore. Instead, we build web applications that might have only one web page and that web page does not represent the layout for our content—it represents a container for our web application. Such a web application with a single web page is called (unsurprisingly) a **Single Page Application** (**SPA**). You might be wondering how do we represent the rest of the content in a SPA? Surely, we need to create an additional layout using HTML tags. Otherwise, how does a web browser know what to render?

These are all valid questions. Let's take a look at how it works. Once you load your web page in a web browser, it creates a **Document Object Model (DOM)** of that web page. A DOM represents your web page in a tree structure, and at this point, it reflects the structure of the layout that you created with HTML tags only. This is what happens regardless of whether you're building a traditional web page or a SPA. The difference between the two is what happens next. If you are building a traditional web page, then you would finish creating your web page's layout. On the other hand, if you are building a SPA, then you would need to start creating additional elements by manipulating the DOM with JavaScript. A web browser provides you with the **JavaScript DOM API** to do this. You can learn more about it at https://developer. mozilla.org/en-US/docs/Web/API/Document_Object_Model.

However, manipulating (or mutating) the DOM with JavaScript has two issues:

- Your programming style will be imperative if you decide to use the JavaScript DOM API directly. As we discussed in the previous chapter, this programming style leads to a code base that is harder to maintain.

- DOM mutations are slow because they cannot be optimized for speed unlike other JavaScript code.

Luckily, React solves both these problems for us.

Understanding the virtual DOM

Why do we need to manipulate the DOM in the first place? It is because our web applications are not static. They have a state represented by a **user interface (UI)** that a web browser renders, and that state can be changed when an event occurs. What kind of events are we talking about? There are two types of events that we're interested in:

- **User events**: When a user types, clicks, scrolls, resizes, and so on

- **Server events**: When an application receives data or an error from a server, among others

What happens while handling these events? Usually, we update the data that our application depends on and that data represents a state of our data model. In turn, when a state of our data model changes, we might want to reflect this change by updating a state of our UI. Looks like what we want is a way of syncing two different states: the UI state and data model state. We want one to react to the changes in the other and vice versa. How can we achieve this?

One of the ways to sync your application's UI state with an underlying data model's state is a two-way data binding. There are different types of two-way data binding. One of them is **Key-Value Observation** (**KVO**), which is used in `Ember.js`, Knockout, Backbone, and iOS, among others. Another one is dirty checking, which is used in Angular.

Instead of a two-way data binding, React offers a different solution called the **virtual DOM**. The virtual DOM is a fast in-memory representation of the real DOM, and it's an abstraction that allows us to treat JavaScript and DOM as if they were reactive. Let's take a look at how it works:

1. Whenever a state of your data model changes, the virtual DOM and React will re-render your UI to a virtual DOM representation.

2. It then calculates the difference between the two virtual DOM representations: the previous virtual DOM representation that was computed before the data was changed and the current virtual DOM representation that was computed after the data was changed. This difference between the two virtual DOM representations is what actually needs to be changed in the real DOM.

3. Update only what needs to be updated in the real DOM.

The process of finding a difference between the two representations of the virtual DOM and re-rendering only the updated patches in a real DOM is fast. Also, the best part is — as a React developer — that you don't need to worry about what actually needs to be re-rendered. React allows you to write your code as if you were re-rendering the entire DOM every time your application's state changes.

If you would like to learn more about the virtual DOM, the rationale behind it, and how it can be compared to data binding, then I would strongly recommend that you watch this very informative talk by Pete Hunt from Facebook at `https://www.youtube.com/watch?v=-DX3vJiqxm4`.

Now that you've learned about the virtual DOM, let's mutate a real DOM by installing React and creating our first React element.

Installing React

To start using the React library, we need to first install it.

At the time of writing, the latest version of React library is 16.0.0. Over time, React gets updated, so make sure that you use the latest version that is available to you, unless it introduces breaking changes that are incompatible with the code samples provided in this book. Visit `https://github.com/PacktPublishing/React-Essentials-Second-Edition` to learn about any compatibility issues between the code samples and the latest version of React.

In *Chapter 2, Installing Powerful Tools for Your Project*, I introduced you to **Webpack**, which allows us to import all the dependency modules for our application using the `import` function. We'll be using `import` to import the React library as well, which means that instead of adding a `<script>` tag to our `index.html` file, we'll be using the `npm install` command to install React:

1. Navigate to the `~/snapterest/` directory and run this command:

   ```
   npm install --save react react-dom
   ```

2. Then, open the `~/snapterest/source/app.js` file in your text editor, and import the React and ReactDOM libraries to the `React` and `ReactDOM` variables, respectively:

   ```
   import React from 'react';
   import ReactDOM from 'react-dom';
   ```

The `react` package contains methods that are concerned with the key idea behind React, that is, describing what you want to render in a declarative way. On the other hand, the `react-dom` package offers methods that are responsible for rendering to the DOM. You can read more about why developers at Facebook think it's a good idea to separate the React library into two packages at `https://facebook.github.io/react/blog/2015/07/03/react-v0.14-beta-1.html#two-packages`.

Now we're ready to start using the React library in our project. Next, let's create our first React element!

Creating React elements with JavaScript

We'll start by familiarizing ourselves with fundamental React terminology. It will help us build a clear picture of what the React library is made of. This terminology will most likely update over time, so keep an eye on the official documentation at `https://facebook.github.io/react/docs/react-api.html`.

Just like the DOM is a tree of nodes, React's virtual DOM is a tree of React nodes. One of the core types in React is called `ReactNode`. It's a building block for a virtual DOM and it can be any one of these core types:

- `ReactElement`: This is the primary type in React. It's a light, stateless, immutable, virtual representation of a `DOMElement`.

- `ReactText`: This is a string or a number. It represents textual content and it's a virtual representation of a text node in the DOM.

`ReactElement` and `ReactText` are `ReactNode`. An array of `ReactNode` is called a `ReactFragment`. You will see examples of all of these in this chapter.

Let's start with an example of `ReactElement`:

1. Add the following code to your `~/snapterest/source/app.js` file:

```
const reactElement = React.createElement('h1');
ReactDOM.render(reactElement,
document.getElementById('react-application'));
```

2. Now your `app.js` file should look exactly like this:

```
import React from 'react';
import ReactDOM from 'react-dom';

const reactElement = React.createElement('h1');
ReactDOM.render(
  reactElement,
  document.getElementById('react-application')
);
```

3. Navigate to the `~/snapterest/` directory and run this command:

npm start

You will see the following output:

Hash: 826f512cf95a44d01d39

Version: webpack 3.8.1

Time: 1851ms

4. Navigate to the ~/snapterest/build/ directory, and open index.html in a web browser. You will see a blank web page. Open **Developer tools** in your web browser and inspect the HTML markup for your blank web page. You should see this line, among others:

```
<h1 data-reactroot></h1>
```

Well done! We've just rendered your first React element. Let's see exactly how we did it.

The entry point to the React library is the React object. This object has a method called createElement() that takes three parameters: type, props, and children:

```
React.createElement(type, props, children);
```

Let's take a look at each parameter in more detail.

The type parameter

The type parameter can be either a string or ReactClass:

- A string could be an HTML tag name, such as 'div', 'p', and 'h1'. React supports all the common HTML tags and attributes. For a complete list of HTML tags and attributes supported by React, you can refer to https://facebook.github.io/react/docs/dom-elements.html.

- A ReactClass class is created via the React.createClass() method. I'll introduce this in more detail in *Chapter 4, Creating Your First React Component*.

The type argument describes how an HTML tag or a ReactClass class is going to be rendered. In our example, we're rendering the h1 HTML tag.

The props parameter

The props parameter is a JavaScript object passed from a parent element to a child element (and not the other way around) with some properties that are considered immutable, that is, those that should not be changed.

While creating DOM elements with React, we can pass the props object with properties that represent the HTML attributes such as class and style. For example, run the following code:

```
import React from 'react';
import ReactDOM from 'react-dom';

const reactElement = React.createElement(
  'h1', { className: 'header' }
```

```
  );
ReactDOM.render(
  reactElement,
  document.getElementById('react-application')
);
```

The preceding code will create an h1 HTML element with a class attribute set to header:

```
<h1 data-reactroot class="header"></h1>
```

Notice that we name our property className rather than class. The reason for this is that the class keyword is reserved in JavaScript. If you use class as a property name, it will be ignored by React, and a helpful warning message will be printed on the web browser's console:

Warning: Unknown DOM property class. Did you mean className?

Use className instead.

You might be wondering what this data-reactroot attribute is doing in our h1 tag? We didn't pass it to our props object, so where did it come from? It is added and used by React to track the DOM nodes.

The children parameter

The children parameter describes what child elements this html element should have, if any. A child element can be any type of ReactNode: a virtual DOM element represented by ReactElement, a string or a number represented by ReactText, or an array of other ReactNode nodes, which is also called ReactFragment.

Let's take a look at this example:

```
import React from 'react';
import ReactDOM from 'react-dom';

const reactElement = React.createElement(
  'h1',
  { className: 'header' },
  'This is React'
);
ReactDOM.render(
  reactElement,
  document.getElementById('react-application')
);
```

The preceding code will create an `h1` HTML element with a `class` attribute and a text node, `This is React`:

```
<h1 data-reactroot class="header">This is React</h1>
```

The `h1` tag is represented by `ReactElement`, while the `This is React` string is represented by `ReactText`.

Next, let's create a React element with a number of other React elements as its children:

```
import React from 'react';
import ReactDOM from 'react-dom';

const h1 = React.createElement(
  'h1',
  { className: 'header', key: 'header' },
  'This is React'
);
const p = React.createElement(
  'p',
  { className: 'content', key: 'content' },
  'And that is how it works.'
);
const reactFragment = [ h1, p ];
const section = React.createElement(
  'section',
  { className: 'container' },
  reactFragment
);

ReactDOM.render(
  section,
  document.getElementById('react-application')
);
```

We've created three React elements: `h1`, `p`, and `section`. The `h1` and `p` both have child text nodes, `'This is React'` and `'And that is how it works.'`, respectively. The `section` tag has a child that is an array of two `ReactElement` types, `h1` and `p`, called `reactFragment`. This is also an array of `ReactNode`. Each `ReactElement` type in the `reactFragment` array must have a `key` property that helps React to identify that `ReactElement` type. As a result, we get the following HTML markup:

```
<section data-reactroot class="container">
  <h1 class="header">This is React</h1>
  <p class="content">And that is how it works.</p>
</section>
```

Now we understand how to create React elements. What if we want to create a number of React elements of the same type? Does it mean that we need to call `React.createElement('type')` over and over again for each element of the same type? We can, but we don't need to because React provides us with a factory function called `React.createFactory()`. A factory function is a function that creates other functions. This is exactly what `React.createFactory(type)` does: it creates a function that produces `ReactElement` of a given type.

Consider the following example:

```
import React from 'react';
import ReactDOM from 'react-dom';

const listItemElement1 = React.createElement(
  'li',
  { className: 'item-1', key: 'item-1' },
  'Item 1'
);
const listItemElement2 = React.createElement(
  'li',
  { className: 'item-2', key: 'item-2' },
  'Item 2'
);
const listItemElement3 = React.createElement(
  'li',
  { className:   'item-3', key: 'item-3' },
  'Item 3'
);

const reactFragment = [
  listItemElement1,
  listItemElement2,
  listItemElement3
];
const listOfItems = React.createElement(
  'ul',
  { className: 'list-of-items' },
  reactFragment
);

ReactDOM.render(
  listOfItems,
  document.getElementById('react-application')
);
```

The preceding example produces this HTML:

```
<ul data-reactroot class="list-of-items">
  <li class="item-1">Item 1</li>
  <li class="item-2">Item 2</li>
  <li class="item-3">Item 3</li>
</ul>
```

We can simplify it by first creating a factory function:

```
import React from 'react';
import ReactDOM from 'react-dom';

const createListItemElement = React.createFactory('li');

const listItemElement1 = createListItemElement(
  { className: 'item-1', key: 'item-1' },
  'Item 1'
);
const listItemElement2 = createListItemElement(
  { className: 'item-2', key: 'item-2' },
  'Item 2'
);
const listItemElement3 = createListItemElement(
  { className: 'item-3', key: 'item-3' },
  'Item 3'
);

const reactFragment = [
  listItemElement1,
  listItemElement2,
  listItemElement3
];
const listOfItems = React.createElement(
  'ul',
  { className: 'list-of-items' },
  reactFragment
);

ReactDOM.render(
  listOfItems,
  document.getElementById('react-application')
);
```

In the preceding example, we're first calling the `React.createFactory()` function and passing a `li` HTML tag name as a type parameter. Then, the `React.createFactory()` function returns a new function that we can use as a convenient shorthand to create elements of the `li` type. We store a reference to this function in a variable called `createListItemElement`. Then, we call this function three times, and each time we only pass the `props` and `children` parameters, which are unique for each element. Notice that `React.createElement()` and `React.createFactory()` both expect an HTML tag name string (such as `li`) or the `ReactClass` object as a type parameter.

React provides us with a number of built-in factory functions to create common HTML tags. You can call them from the `React.DOM` object; for example, `React.DOM.ul()`, `React.DOM.li()`, and `React.DOM.div()`. Using them, we can simplify our previous example even further:

```
import React from 'react';
import ReactDOM from 'react-dom';

const listItemElement1 = React.DOM.li(
  { className: 'item-1', key: 'item-1' },
  'Item 1'
);
const listItemElement2 = React.DOM.li(
  { className: 'item-2', key: 'item-2' },
  'Item 2'
);
const listItemElement3 = React.DOM.li(
  { className: 'item-3', key: 'item-3' },
  'Item 3'
);

const reactFragment = [
  listItemElement1,
  listItemElement2,
  listItemElement3
];
const listOfItems = React.DOM.ul(
  { className: 'list-of-items' },
  reactFragment
);

ReactDOM.render(
  listOfItems,
  document.getElementById('react-application')
);
```

Now, we know how to create a tree of `ReactNode`. However, there is one important line of code that we need to discuss before we can progress further:

```
ReactDOM.render(
  listOfItems,
  document.getElementById('react-application')
);
```

As you might have already guessed, it renders our `ReactNode` tree to the DOM. Let's take a closer look at how it works.

Rendering React elements

The `ReactDOM.render()` method takes three parameters: `ReactElement`, a regular `DOMElement` container, and a `callback` function:

```
ReactDOM.render(ReactElement, DOMElement, callback);
```

A `ReactElement` type is a root element in the tree of `ReactNode` that you've created. A regular `DOMElement` parameter is a container DOM node for that tree. The `callback` parameter is a function executed after the tree is rendered or updated. It's important to note that if this `ReactElement` type was previously rendered to a parent `DOMElement` container, then `ReactDOM.render()` will perform an update on the already rendered DOM tree and only mutate the DOM, as it is necessary to reflect the latest version of the `ReactElement` type. This is why a virtual DOM requires fewer DOM mutations.

So far, we've assumed that we're always creating our virtual DOM in a web browser. This is understandable because, after all, React is a user interface library, and all user interfaces are rendered in a web browser. Can you think of a case when rendering a user interface on a client would be slow? Some of you might have already guessed that I am talking about the initial page load. The problem with the initial page load is the one I mentioned at the beginning of this chapter — we're not creating static web pages anymore. Instead, when a web browser loads our web application, it receives only the bare minimum HTML markup that is usually used as a container or a parent element for our web application. Then, our JavaScript code creates the rest of the DOM, but in order for it to do so, it often needs to request extra data from the server. However, getting this data takes time. Once this data is received, our JavaScript code starts to mutate the DOM. We know that DOM mutations are slow. How can we solve this problem?

The solution is somewhat unexpected. Instead of mutating the DOM in a web browser, we mutate it on a server, just like we would with our static web pages. A web browser will then receive an HTML that fully represents a user interface of our web application at the time of the initial page load. Sounds simple, but we can't mutate the DOM on a server because it doesn't exist outside a web browser. Or can we?

We have a virtual DOM that is just JavaScript, and using Node.js, we can run JavaScript on a server. So, technically, we can use the React library on a server, and we can create our `ReactNode` tree on a server. The question is how can we render it to a string that we can send to a client?

React has a method called `ReactDOMServer.renderToString()` just to do this:

```
import ReactDOMServer from 'react-dom/server';
ReactDOMServer.renderToString(ReactElement);
```

The `ReactDOMServer.renderToString()` method takes `ReactElement` as a parameter and renders it to its initial HTML. Not only is this faster than mutating a DOM on a client, but it also improves the **Search Engine Optimization (SEO)** of your web application.

Speaking of generating static web pages, we can do this too with React:

```
import ReactDOMServer from 'react-dom/server';
ReactDOMServer.renderToStaticMarkup(ReactElement);
```

Similar to `ReactDOMServer.renderToString()`, this method also takes `ReactElement` as a parameter and outputs an HTML string. However, it doesn't create extra DOM attributes that React uses internally, producing shorter HTML strings that we can transfer to the wire quickly.

Now you know not only how to create a virtual DOM tree using React elements, but you also know how to render it to a client and server. Our next question is whether we can do it quickly and in a more visual manner.

Creating React elements with JSX

When we build our virtual DOM by constantly calling the `React.createElement()` method, it becomes quite hard to translate these multiple function calls visually into a hierarchy of HTML tags. Don't forget that even though we're working with a virtual DOM, we're still creating a structure layout for our content and user interface. Wouldn't it be great to be able to visualize that layout easily by simply looking at our React code?

JSX is an optional HTML-like syntax that allows us to create a virtual DOM tree, without using the `React.createElement()` method.

Let's take a look at the previous example that we created without JSX:

```
import React from 'react';
import ReactDOM from 'react-dom';

const listItemElement1 = React.DOM.li(
  { className: 'item-1', key: 'item-1' },
  'Item 1'
);
const listItemElement2 = React.DOM.li(
  { className: 'item-2', key: 'item-2' },
  'Item 2'
);
const listItemElement3 = React.DOM.li(
  { className: 'item-3', key: 'item-3' },
  'Item 3'
);

const reactFragment = [
  listItemElement1,
  listItemElement2,
  listItemElement3
];
const listOfItems = React.DOM.ul(
  { className: 'list-of-items' },
  reactFragment
);

ReactDOM.render(
  listOfItems,
  document.getElementById('react-application')
);
```

Translate this into the one with JSX:

```
import React from 'react';
import ReactDOM from 'react-dom';

const listOfItems = (
  <ul className="list-of-items">
    <li className="item-1">Item 1</li>
    <li className="item-2">Item 2</li>
    <li className="item-3">Item 3</li>
  </ul>
```

```
);

ReactDOM.render(
  listOfItems,
  document.getElementById('react-application')
);
```

As you can see, JSX allows us to write HTML-like syntax in our JavaScript code. More importantly, we can now clearly see what our HTML layout will look like once it's rendered. JSX is a convenience tool and it comes with a price in the form of an additional transformation step. A transformation of JSX syntax into a valid JavaScript syntax must happen before our "invalid" JavaScript code is interpreted.

In our previous chapter, we installed the `babel-preset-react` module that transforms our JSX syntax into valid JavaScript. This transformation happens every time we run Webpack. Navigate to `~/snapterest/` and run this command:

npm start

Now navigate to the `~/snapterest/build/` directory, and open `index.html` in a web browser. You will see a list of three items. The result is the same, only this time you've used JSX to create this HTML markup.

To understand JSX syntax better, I recommend that you play with the Babel REPL tool: `https://babeljs.io/repl/` — it converts your JSX syntax to plain JavaScript on the fly.

Using JSX, you might feel very unusual in the beginning, but it can become a very intuitive and convenient tool to use. The best part is that you can choose whether to use it or not. I found that JSX saves me development time, so I chose to use it in this project that we're building.

If you have a question about what we discussed in this chapter, then you can refer to `https://github.com/fedosejev/react-essentials` and create a new issue.

Summary

We started this chapter by discussing the issues with single web page applications and how they can be addressed. Then, you learned what a virtual DOM is and how React allows us to build one. We also installed React and created our first React element using only JavaScript. Then, you also learned how to render React elements in a web browser and on a server. Finally, we looked at a simpler way of creating React elements with JSX.

In the next chapter, we'll dive deeper into the world of React components.

4
Creating Your First React Component

In the previous chapter, you learned how to create React elements and how to use them to render the HTML markup. You saw how easy it is to produce React elements using JSX. At this point, you know enough about React to create static web pages, which we discussed in *Chapter 3, Creating Your First React Element*. However, I bet that's not the reason why you've decided to learn React. You don't want to just build websites made of static HTML elements. You want to build interactive user interfaces that react to user and server events. What does it mean to react to an event? How can a static HTML element **react**? How can a React element react? In this chapter, we'll answer these questions and many other questions while introducing ourselves to React components.

Stateless versus stateful

To react means to switch from one state to another. This means that you need to have a state in the first place and the ability to change that state. Have we mentioned a state or the ability to change that state in React elements? No. They are stateless. Their sole purpose is to construct and render virtual DOM elements. In fact, we want them to render in the exact same way, given that we provide them with exactly the same set of parameters. We want them to be consistent because it makes it easy for us to reason about them. This is one of the key benefits of using React—the ease of reasoning about how our web application works.

How can we add state to our stateless React elements? If we can't encapsulate state in React elements, then we should encapsulate React elements in something that already has state. Think of a simple state machine that represents a user interface. Every user action triggers a change of a state in that state machine. Every state is represented by a different React element. In React, this state machine is called a **React component**.

Creating your first stateless React component

Let's take a look at the following example of how to create a React component:

```
import React, { Component } from 'react';
import ReactDOM from 'react-dom';

class ReactClass extends Component {
  render () {
    return (
      <h1 className="header">React Component</h1>
    );
  }
}

const reactComponent = ReactDOM.render(
  <ReactClass/>,
  document.getElementById('react-application')
);
export default ReactClass;
```

Some of the preceding code should already look familiar to you, and the rest can be broken down into two simple steps:

1. Creating a React component class.
2. Creating a React component.

Let's take a closer look at how we can create a React component:

1. Create a `ReactClass` class as a subclass of the `Component` class. In this chapter, we'll focus on learning how to create React component classes in more detail.

2. Create `reactComponent` by calling the `ReactDOM.render()` function and providing our `ReactClass` element as its element parameter.

I strongly recommend that you read this blog post by Dan Abramov that explains in greater details the differences between React components, elements and instances: `https://facebook.github.io/react/blog/2015/12/18/react-components-elements-and-instances.html`

The look and feel of our React component is declared in `ReactClass`.

The `Component` class encapsulates a component's state and describes how a component is rendered. At the very minimum, the React component class needs to have a `render()` method so that it returns `null` or `false`. Here is an example of a `render()` method in its simplest form:

```
class ReactClass extends Component {
  render() {
    return null;
  }
}
```

As you can guess, the `render()` method is responsible for telling React what this component should render. It can return `null`, as in the preceding example, and nothing will be rendered on the screen. Or, it can return JSX elements that we learned how to create in *Chapter 3, Creating Your First React Element*:

```
class ReactClass extends Component {
  render() {
    return (
      <h1 className="header">React Component</h1>
    );
  }
}
```

This example shows how we can encapsulate our React element inside our React component. We create an `h1` element with a `className` property and some text as its children. Then, we return it when the `render()` method is called. The fact that we encapsulated our React element inside a React component doesn't affect how it will be rendered:

```
<h1 data-reactroot class="header">React Component</h1>
```

As you can see, the produced HTML markup is identical to the one we created in *Chapter 3, Creating Your First React Element*, without using the React component. In this case, you might be wondering, what's the benefit of having a `render()` method if we can render the exact same markup without it?

The advantage of having a render() method is that, like with any other function, before it returns a value, it can choose what value to return. So far, you've seen two examples of a render() method: one that returns null and the other one that returns a React element. We can merge the two and add a condition that decides what to render:

```
class ReactClass extends Component {
  render() {
    const componentState = {
      isHidden: true
    };

    if (componentState.isHidden) {
      return null;
    }

    return (
      <h1 className="header">React Component</h1>
    );
  }
}
```

In this example, we created the componentState constant that references to an object with a single isHidden property. This object acts as a state for our React component. If we want to hide our React component, then we need to set the value of componentState.isHidden to true, and our render function will return null. In this case, React will render nothing. Logically, setting componentState.isHidden to false, will return our React element and render the expected HTML markup. The question you might ask is how do we set the value of componentState.isHidden to false? Or to true? Or how do we change it in general?

Let's think of scenarios in which we might want to change that state. One of them is when a user interacts with our user interface. Another one is when a server sends data. Or, when a certain amount of time passes, and now, we want to render something else. Our render() method is not aware of all these events, and it shouldn't be because its sole purpose is to return a React element based on the data that we pass to it. How do we pass data to it?

There are two ways to pass data to a render() method using the React API:

- this.props
- this.state

Here, `this.props` should look familiar to you. In *Chapter 3, Creating Your First React Element,* you learned that the `React.createElement()` function accepts the `props` parameter. We used it to pass attributes to our HTML elements, but we didn't discuss what happens behind the scene and why attributes passed to the `props` object get rendered.

Any data that you put in the `props` object and pass to JSX elements can be accessed inside the `render()` method via `this.props`. Once you access data from `this.props`, you can render it:

```
class ReactClass extends Component {
  render() {
    const componentState = {
      isHidden: false
    };

    if (componentState.isHidden) {
      return null;
    }

    return (
      <h1 className="header">{this.props.header}</h1>
    );
  }
}
```

In this example, we're using `this.props` inside of our `render()` method to access the `header` property. We're then passing `this.props.header` directly to the `h1` element as a child.

In the preceding example, we can pass the value of `isHidden` as another property of the `this.props` object:

```
class ReactClass extends Component {
  render() {
    if (this.props.isHidden) {
      return null;
    }

    return (
      <h1 className="header">{this.props.header}</h1>
    );
  }
}
```

Notice that in this example we're repeating `this.props` twice. It's quite common for a `this.props` object to have properties that we want to access multiple times in our `render` method. For this reason, I recommend that you destructure `this.props` first:

```
class ReactClass extends Component {
  render() {
    const {
      isHidden,
      header
    } = this.props;

    if (isHidden) {
      return null;
    }

    return (
      <h1 className="header">{this.header}</h1>
    );
  }
}
```

Have you noticed how in the previous example instead of storing `isHidden` in a `render()` method we're passing it via `this.props`? We removed our `componentState` object because we don't need to worry about the component's state in our `render()` method. The `render()` method shouldn't mutate the component's state or access the real DOM or otherwise interact with a web browser. We might want to render our React component on a server, where we have no web browser, and we should expect the `render()` method to produce the same result regardless of the environment.

If our `render()` method doesn't manage the state, then how do we manage it? How do we set the state, and how do we update it while handling user or browser events in React?

Earlier in this chapter, you learned that in React, we can represent a user interface with React components. There are two types of React components:

- With a state
- Without a state

Hold on! Didn't we say that React components are state machines? Surely, every state machine needs to have a state. You're correct, however, it's a good practice to keep as many React components stateless as possible.

React components are composable. As a result, we can have a hierarchy of React components. Imagine that we have a parent React component that has two child components, and each of them in turn has another two child components. All the components are stateful and they can manage their own state:

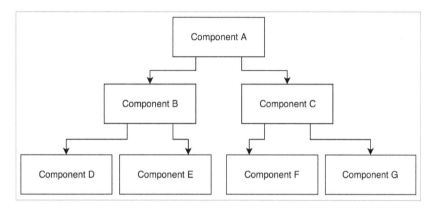

How easy will it be to figure out what the last child component in the hierarchy will render, if the top component in the hierarchy updates its state? Not easy. There is a design pattern that removes this unnecessary complexity. The idea is to separate your components by two concerns: how to handle the user interface interaction logic and how to render data.

- The minority of your React components are stateful. They should be at the top of your components' hierarchy. They encapsulate all of the interaction logic, manage the user interface state, and pass that state down the hierarchy to stateless components using `props`.
- The majority of your React components are stateless. They receive their parent components' state data via `this.props` and render that data accordingly.

In our previous example, we received the `isHidden` state data via `this.props`, and then we rendered that data. Our component was stateless.

Next, let's create our first stateful component.

Creating your first stateful React component

Stateful components are the most appropriate place for your application to handle the interaction logic and manage states. They make it easier for you to reason about how your application works. This reasoning plays a key role in building maintainable web applications.

React stores the component's state in a `this.state` object. We assign the initial value of `this.state` as a public class field of the `Component` class:

```
class ReactClass extends React.Component {
  state = {
    isHidden: false
  };

  render() {
    const {
      isHidden
    } = this.state;

    if (isHidden) {
      return null;
    }

    return (
      <h1 className="header">React Component</h1>
    );
  }
}
```

Now, `{ isHidden: false }` is the initial state of our React component and our user interface. Notice that in our `render()` method, we're now destructuring the `isHidden` property from `this.state` instead of `this.props`.

Earlier in this chapter, you learned that we can pass data to the component's `render()` function via `this.props` or `this.state`. What is the difference between the two?

- `this.props`: This stores read-only data that is passed from the parent. It belongs to the parent and cannot be changed by its children. This data should be considered immutable.

- `this.state`: This stores data that is private to the component. It can be changed by the component. The component will re-render itself when the state is updated.

How do we update a component's state? You can inform React of a state change using `setState(nextState, callback)`. This function takes two parameters:

- The `nextState` object that represents the next state. It could also be a function with a signature of `function(prevState, props) => newState`. This function takes two parameters: previous state and properties, and returns an object that represents a new state.

- The `callback` function, which you will rarely need to use because React keeps your user interface up to date for you.

How does React keep your user interface up to date? It calls the component's `render()` function every time you update the component's state, including any child components, which are re-rendered as well. In fact, it re-renders the entire virtual DOM every time our `render()` function is called.

When you call the `this.setState()` function and pass it a data object that represents the next state, React will merge that next state with the current state. During the merge, React will overwrite the current state with the next state. The current state that is not overwritten by the next state will become part of the next state.

Imagine that this is our current state:

```
{
  isHidden: true,
  title: 'Stateful React Component'
}
```

We call `this.setState(nextState)`, where `nextState` is as follows:

```
{
  isHidden: false
}
```

React will merge the two states into a new one:

```
{
  isHidden: false,
  title: 'Stateful React Component'
}
```

The `isHidden` property was updated and the `title` property was not deleted or updated in any way.

Now that we know how to update our component's state, let's create a stateful component that reacts to a user event:

In this example, we're creating a toggle button that shows and hides a header. The first thing we do is that we set our initial state object. Our initial state has two properties: isHeaderHidden that is set to false, and the title set to Stateful React Component. Now, we can access this state object in our render() method via this.state. Inside our render() method, we create three React elements: h1, button, and div. Our div element acts as a parent element for our h1 and button elements. However, in one case, we create our div element with two children, the header and button elements, and in another case, we create it with only one child, the button. The case we choose depends on the value of this.state. isHeaderHidden. The current state of our component directly affects what the render() function will render. While this should look familiar to you, there is something new in this example that we haven't seen before.

Notice that we've added a new method called handleClick() to our component class. The handleClick() method has no special meaning to React. It's part of our application logic, and we use it to handle the onClick events. You can add your own custom methods to a React component class as well because it's just a JavaScript class. All of these methods will be available via a this reference, which you can access in any method in your component class. For example, we are accessing a state object via this.state in both the render() and handleClick() methods.

What does our handleClick() method do? It updates our component's state by toggling the isHeaderHidden property:

```
this.setState(prevState => ({
  isHeaderHidden: !prevState.isHeaderHidden
}));
```

Our handleClick() method reacts to a user's interaction with our user interface. Our user interface is a button element that a user can click on, and we can attach an event handler to it. In React, you can attach event handlers to components by passing them to JSX properties:

```
<button onClick={this.handleClick}>
  Toggle Header
</button>
```

React uses the **camelCase** naming convention for event handlers, for example, onClick. You can find a list of all the supported events at http://facebook. github.io/react/docs/events.html#supported-events.

By default, React triggers the event handlers in the bubble phase, but you can tell React to trigger them in the capture phase by appending Capture to the event name, for example, onClickCapture.

React wraps a browser's native events into the `SyntheticEvent` object to ensure that all the supported events behave identically in Internet Explorer 8 and above.

The `SyntheticEvent` object provides the same API as the native browser's event, which means that you can use the `stopPropagation()` and `preventDefault()` methods as usual. If for some reason, you need to access that native browser's event, then you can do this via the `nativeEvent` property.

Notice that passing the `onClick` property to our `createElement()` function in the previous example does not create an inline event handler in the rendered HTML markup:

```
<button class="btn btn-default">Toggle header</button>
```

This is because React doesn't actually attach event handlers to the DOM nodes themselves. Instead, React listens for all the events at the top level using a single event listener and delegates them to their appropriate event handlers.

In the previous example, you learned how to create a stateful React component that a user can interact with and change its state. We created and attached an event handler to the `click` event that updates the value of the `isHeaderHidden` property. But have you noticed that the user interaction does not update the value of another property that we store in our state, `title`. Does that seem odd to you? We have data in our state that doesn't ever get changed. This observation raises an important question; what should we *not* put in our state?

Ask yourself, "What data can I remove from a component's state and still keep its user interface always up to date?" Keep asking and keep removing that data until you're absolutely certain that there is nothing left to remove, without breaking your user interface.

In our example, we have the `title` property in our state object that we can move to our `render()` method, without breaking the interactivity of our toggle button. The component will still work as expected:

```
class ReactClass extends Component {
  state = {
    isHeaderHidden: false
  }

  handleClick = () => {
    this.setState(prevState => ({
      isHeaderHidden: !prevState.isHeaderHidden
    }));
  }
```

```
render() {
  const {
    isHeaderHidden
  } = this.state;

  if (isHeaderHidden) {
    return (
      <button
        className="btn ban-default"
        onClick={this.handleClick}
      >
        Toggle Header
      </button>
    );
  }

  return (
    <div>
      <h1 className="header">Stateful React Component</h1>
      <button
        className="btn ban-default"
        onClick={this.handleClick}
      >
        Toggle Header
      </button>
    </div>
  );
  }
}
```

On the other hand, if we move the isHeaderHidden property out of our state object, then we'll break the interactivity of our component, because our render() method will not be triggered automatically by React every time that a user clicks on our button anymore. This is an example of broken interactivity:

```
class ReactClass extends Component {
  state = {}
  isHeaderHidden = false

  handleClick = () => {
    this.isHeaderHidden = !this.isHeaderHidden;
  }

  render() {
    if (this.isHeaderHidden) {
      return (
        <button
```

```
          className="btn ban-default"
          onClick={this.handleClick}
        >
          Toggle Header
        </button>
      );
    }

    return (
      <div>
        <h1 className="header">Stateful React Component</h1>
        <button
          className="btn ban-default"
          onClick={this.handleClick}
        >
          Toggle Header
        </button>
      </div>
    );
  }
}
```

 Note: For better results in the output, please refer to the code files.

This is an antipattern.

Remember this rule of thumb: a component's state should store data that a component's event handlers may change over time in order to re-render a component's user interface and keep it up to date. Keep the minimal possible representation of a component's state in a `state` object, and compute the rest of the data based on what's in `state` and `props` inside a component's `render()` method. Take advantage of the fact that React will re-render your component when its state is changed.

Summary

In this chapter, you reached an important milestone: you learned how to encapsulate a state and create interactive user interfaces by creating React components. We discussed stateless and stateful React components and the difference, between them. We talked about browser events and how to handle them in React.

In the next chapter, you'll learn what's new in React 16.

5
Making Your React Components Reactive

Now that you know how to create React components with and without state, we can start composing React components together and build more complex user interfaces. In fact, it's time for us to start building our web application called **Snapterest** that we discussed in *Chapter 2, Installing Powerful Tools for Your Project*. While doing this, you'll learn how to plan your React application and create composable React components. Let's begin.

Solving a problem using React

Before you start writing code for your web application, you need to think about the problems that your web application is going to solve. It's very important to understand that to define the problem as clearly and as early as possible is the most important step toward a successful solution—a useful web application. If you failed to define your problem earlier in your development process, or you defined it inaccurately, then later on you'll have to stop, rethink what you're doing, throw away a piece of the code that you have already written, and write a new one. This is a wasteful approach, and as a professional software developer, your time is very valuable not only to you but also to your organization, so it's in your best interest to invest it wisely. Earlier in this book, I stressed the fact that one of the benefits of using React is code reuse, which means that you'll be able to do more in less time. However, before we take a look at the React code, let's first discuss the problem, keeping React in mind.

We'll be building Snapterest—a web application that receives tweets from a Snapkite Engine server in a real-time manner and displays them one at a time to a user. We don't actually know when Snapterest will receive a new tweet, but when it does, it will display that new tweet for at least 1.5 seconds so that the user has enough time to take a look at it, and click on it. Clicking on a tweet will add it to an existing collection of tweets or create a new one. Finally, users will be able to export their collection to HTML markup code.

This is a very high-level description of what we're going to build. Let's break it down into a list of smaller tasks:

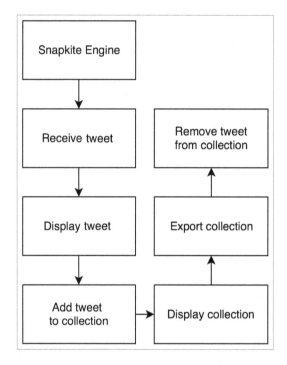

The following are the steps:

1. Receive tweets from the Snapkite Engine server in real time.
2. Display one tweet at a time for at least 1.5 seconds.
3. Add tweets to a collection on a user click event.
4. Display a list of tweets in a collection.
5. Create HTML markup code for a collection and export it.
6. Remove tweets from a collection, on a user click event.

Can you identify which tasks can be solved using React? Remember that React is a user interface library, so anything that describes the user interface and interactions with that user interface can be addressed with React. In the preceding list, React can take care of all the tasks, except for the first one because it describes data fetching and not the user interface. Step 1 will be solved with another library that we'll discuss in the next chapter. Steps 2 and 4 describe something that needs to be displayed. They are perfect candidates for React components. Steps 3 and 6 describe the user events, and as we've seen in *Chapter 4*, *Creating Your First React Component*, the handling of user events handling can be encapsulated in React components as well. Can you think of how step 5 can be solved with React? Remember in *Chapter 3*, *Creating Your First React Element*, we discussed the `ReactDOMServer.renderToStaticMarkup()` method that renders the React element to a static HTML markup string. This is exactly what we need in order to solve step 5.

Now when we've identified a potential solution for each individual task, let's think about how we are going to put them together and create a fully functional web application.

There are two ways to build composable React applications:

*   First, you can start by building individual React components, and then compose them together into higher-level React components, moving up the component hierarchy
*   You can start from the topmost React element and then implement its child components, moving down the component hierarchy

The second strategy has an advantage of seeing and understanding the big picture of your application's architecture, and I think it's important to understand how everything fits together before we can think of how individual pieces of functionality are implemented.

Planning your React application

There are two simple guidelines we need to follow when planning your React application:

*   Each React component should represent a single user interface element in your web application. It should encapsulate the smallest element possible that can potentially be reused.

- Multiple React components should be composed into a single React component. Ultimately, your entire user interface should be encapsulated in one React component.

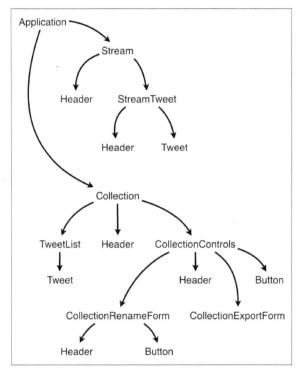

Diagram of our React components hierarchy

We'll begin with our topmost React component, **Application**. It will encapsulate our entire React application, and it will have two child components: the **Stream** and **Collection** components. The **Stream** component will be responsible for connecting to a stream of tweets, receiving, and displaying the latest tweet. The **Stream** component will have two child components: **StreamTweet** and **Header**. The **StreamTweet** component will be responsible for displaying the latest tweet. It will be composed of the **Header** and **Tweet** components. A **Header** component will render a header. It will have no child components. A **Tweet** component will render an image from a tweet. Notice how we're planning to reuse the **Header** component twice already.

The **Collection** component will be responsible for displaying the collection controls and a list of tweets. It will have two child components: **CollectionControls** and **TweetList**. The **CollectionControls** component will have two child components: the **CollectionRenameForm** component that will render a form to rename a collection, and the **CollectionExportForm** component that will render a form to export a collection to a service called **CodePen**, which is an HTML, CSS, and JavaScript playground website. You can learn more about CodePen at `http://codepen.io`. As you might have noticed, we'll reuse the **Header** and **Button** components in the **CollectionRenameForm** and **CollectionControls** components. Our **TweetList** component will render a list of tweets. Each tweet will be rendered by a **Tweet** component. We'll be reusing the **Header** component once again in our **Collection** component. In fact, in total, we'll be reusing the **Header** component five times. That's a win for us. As we discussed in the previous chapter, we should keep as many React components stateless as possible. So only 5 out of 11 components will store the state, which are as follows:

- **Application**
- **CollectionControls**
- **CollectionRenameForm**
- **Stream**
- **StreamTweet**

Now when we have a plan, we can start implementing it.

Creating a container React component

Let's start by editing our application's main JavaScript file. Replace the content of the `~/snapterest/source/app.js` file with the following code snippet:

```
import React from 'react';
import ReactDOM from 'react-dom';
import Application from './components/Application';

ReactDOM.render(
  <Application />,
  document.getElementById('react-application')
);
```

There are only four lines of code in this file, and as you can guess, they provide
`document.getElementById('react-application')` as a deployment target for the
`<Application/>` component and render `<Application/>` to the DOM. The whole
user interface for our web application will be encapsulated in one React component,
`Application`.

Next, navigate to `~/snapterest/source/components/` and create the
`Application.js` file inside this directory:

```js
import React, { Component } from 'react';
import Stream from './Stream';
import Collection from './Collection';

class Application extends Component {
  state = {
    collectionTweets: {}
  }

  addTweetToCollection = (tweet) => {
    const { collectionTweets } = this.state;

    collectionTweets[tweet.id] = tweet;

    this.setState({
      collectionTweets: collectionTweets
    });
  }

  removeTweetFromCollection = (tweet) => {
    const { collectionTweets } = this.state;

    delete collectionTweets[tweet.id];

    this.setState({
      collectionTweets: collectionTweets
    });
  }

  removeAllTweetsFromCollection = () => {
    this.setState({
      collectionTweets: {}
    });
  }
```

```
  render() {
    const {
      addTweetToCollection,
      removeTweetFromCollection,
      removeAllTweetsFromCollection
    } = this;

    return (
      <div className="container-fluid">
        <div className="row">
          <div className="col-md-4 text-center">
            <Stream onAddTweetToCollection=
            {addTweetToCollection}/>
          </div>
          <div className="col-md-8">
            <Collection
              tweets={this.state.collectionTweets}
              onRemoveTweetFromCollection=
              {removeTweetFromCollection}
              onRemoveAllTweetsFromCollection=
              {removeAllTweetsFromCollection}
            />
          </div>
        </div>
      </div>
    );
  }
}

export default Application;
```

This component has significantly more code than our app.js file, but this code can be easily divided into three logical parts:

- Importing dependency modules
- Defining a React component class
- Exporting a React component class as a module

In our first logical part of the Application.js file, we're importing the dependency modules using the require() function:

```
import React, { Component } from 'react';
import Stream from './Stream';
import Collection from './Collection';
```

Our `Application` component will have two child components that we need to import:

- The `Stream` component will render a stream section of our user interface
- The `Collection` component will render a collection section of our user interface

We also need to import the `React` library as another module.

The second logical part of the `Application.js` file creates the React `Application` component class with the following methods:

- `addTweetToCollection()`
- `removeTweetFromCollection()`
- `removeAllTweetsFromCollection()`
- `render()`

Only the `render()` method is part of the React API. All the other methods are part of our application logic that this component encapsulates. We'll take a closer look at each of them right after we discuss what this component renders inside its `render()` method:

```
render() {
  const {
    addTweetToCollection,
    removeTweetFromCollection,
    removeAllTweetsFromCollection
  } = this;

  return (
    <div className="container-fluid">
      <div className="row">
        <div className="col-md-4 text-center">
          <Stream onAddTweetToCollection={addTweetToCollection}/>
        </div>
        <div className="col-md-8">
          <Collection
            tweets={this.state.collectionTweets}
            onRemoveTweetFromCollection=
            {removeTweetFromCollection}
            onRemoveAllTweetsFromCollection=
            {removeAllTweetsFromCollection}
          />
        </div>
```

```
        </div>
      </div>
    );
  }
```

As you can see, it defines the layout of our web page using the Bootstrap framework. If you're not familiar with Bootstrap, I strongly recommend that you visit http:// getbootstrap.com and read the documentation. Learning this framework will empower you to prototype user interfaces quickly and easily. Even if you don't know Bootstrap, it's quite easy to understand what's going on. We're dividing our web page into two columns: a smaller one and a larger one. The smaller one contains our `Stream` React component, and the larger one contains our `Collection` component. You can imagine that our web page is divided into two unequal parts, and both of them contain the React components.

This is how we're using our `Stream` component:

```
<Stream onAddTweetToCollection={addTweetToCollection} />
```

The `Stream` component has an `onAddTweetToCollection` property and our `Application` component passes its own `addTweetToCollection()` method as a value for this property. The `addTweetToCollection()` method adds a tweet to a collection. It's one of the custom methods that we define in our `Application` component. We don't need the `this` keyword because the method was defined as an arrow function, so the scope of the function is automatically our component.

Let's take a look at what the `addTweetToCollection()` method does:

```
addTweetToCollection = (tweet) => {
  const { collectionTweets } = this.state;

  collectionTweets[tweet.id] = tweet;

  this.setState({
    collectionTweets: collectionTweets
  });
}
```

This method references collection tweets that are stored in the current state, adds a new tweet to a `collectionTweets` object, and updates the state by calling the `setState()` method. A new tweet is passed as an argument when the `addTweetToCollection()` method is called inside a `Stream` component. This is an example of how a child component can update its parent component's state.

This an important mechanism in React and it works as follows:

1. A parent component passes a callback function as a property to its child component. A child component can access this callback function via the `this.props` reference.

2. Whenever a child component wants to update the parent component's state, it calls that callback function and passes all the necessary data to a new parent component's state.

3. A parent component updates its state, and as you already know that this state updates and triggers the `render()` method that re-renders all the child components as necessary.

This is how a child component interacts with a parent component. This interaction allows a child component to delegate the application's state management to its parent component, and it is only concerned with how to render itself. Now when you've learned this pattern, you will be using it again and again because most of your React components should stay stateless. Only a few parent components should store and manage your application's state. This best practice allows us to logically group React components by two different concerns that they address:

- Managing the application's state and rendering it
- Only rendering and delegating the application's state management to a parent component

Our `Application` component has a second child component, `Collection`:

```
<Collection
    tweets={this.state.collectionTweets}
    onRemoveTweetFromCollection={removeTweetFromCollection}
    onRemoveAllTweetsFromCollection={removeAllTweetsFromCollection}
/>
```

This component has a number of properties:

- `tweets`: This refers to our current collection of tweets
- `onRemoveTweetFromCollection`: This refers to a function that removes a particular tweet from our collection
- `onRemoveAllTweetsFromCollection`: This refers to a function that removes all the tweets from our collection

You can see that the `Collection` component's properties are only concerned about how to do the following:

- Access the application's state
- Mutate the application's state

As you can guess, the `onRemoveTweetFromCollection` and `onRemoveAllTweetsFromCollection` functions allow the `Collection` component to mutate the `Application` component's state. On the other hand, the `tweets` property propagates the `Application` component's state to the `Collection` component so that it can gain read-only access to that state.

Can you recognize the single direction of data flow between the `Application` and `Collection` components? Here's how it works:

1. The `collectionTweets` data is initialized in the `Application` component's `constructor()` method.
2. The `collectionTweets` data is passed to the `Collection` component as the `tweets` property.
3. The `Collection` component calls the `removeTweetFromCollection` and `removeAllTweetsFromCollection` functions that update the `collectionTweets` data in the `Application` component, and the cycle starts again.

Notice that the `Collection` component cannot directly mutate the `Application` component's state. The `Collection` component has read-only access to that state via a `this.props` object, and the only way to update the parent component's state is to call the callback functions that are passed by a parent component. In the `Collection` component, these callback functions are `this.props.onRemoveTweetFromCollection` and `this.props.onRemoveAllTweetsFromCollection`.

This simple mental model of how data flows in our React component hierarchy will help us increase the number of components we use, without increasing the complexity of how our user interface works. For example, it can have upto 10 levels of nested React components, as follows:

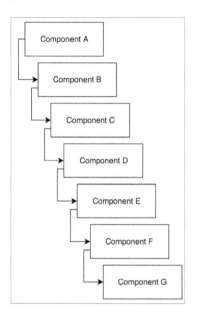

If Component G wants to mutate the state of root Component A, it would do it in exactly the same way as Component B or Component F, or as any other component in this hierarchy would. However, in React, you shouldn't pass data from Component A directly to Component G. Instead, you should first pass it to Component B, then to Component C, then to Component D, and so on, until you finally reach Component G. Component B to Component F will have to carry some "transit" properties that are actually only meant for Component G. This might look like a waste of time, but this design makes it easy for us to debug our application and reason out how it works. There are always strategies to optimize your application's architecture. One of them is to use **Flux design pattern**. Another one is to use **Redux** library. We'll discuss both later in this book.

Before we finish discussing our Application component, let's take a look at the two methods that mutate its state:

```
removeTweetFromCollection = (tweet) => {
  const { collectionTweets } = this.state;

  delete collectionTweets[tweet.id];
```

```
    this.setState({
       collectionTweets: collectionTweets
    });
  }
```

The `removeTweetFromCollection()` method removes a tweet from a collection of tweets that we store in the `Application` component's state. It takes the current `collectionTweets` object from the component's state, deletes a tweet with a given `id` from that object, and updates the component's state with an updated `collectionTweets` object.

On the other hand, the `removeAllTweetsFromCollection()` method removes all the tweets from the component's state:

```
  removeAllTweetsFromCollection = () => {
    this.setState({
      collectionTweets: {}
    });
  }
```

Both of these methods are called from a child's `Collection` component because that component has no other way to mutate the `Application` component's state.

Summary

In this chapter, you learned how to solve a problem with React. We started by breaking down the problem into smaller individual problems and then discussing how we can address them using React. Then, we created a list of React components that we will need to implement. Finally, we created our first composable React component and learned about how a parent component interacts with its child components.

In the next chapter, we'll implement our child components and learn about React's life cycle methods.

6
Using Your React Components with Another Library

React is a great library for building user interfaces. What if we want to integrate it with another library that is responsible for receiving data? In the previous chapter, we outlined five tasks that our Snapterest web application should be able to perform. We decided that four of them were related to the user interface, but one of them was all about receiving data: receiving tweets from the Snapkite Engine server in real time.

In this chapter, you'll learn how to integrate React with the external JavaScript library and what React component lifecycle methods are, all while solving the important task of receiving data.

Using another library in your React component

As we discussed earlier in this book, our Snapterest web application will consume a live stream of tweets. In *Chapter 2, Installing Powerful Tools for Your Project*, you installed the **Snapkite Engine** library that connects to the Twitter Streaming API, filters incoming tweets, and sends them to our client application. In turn, our client application needs a way of connecting to that live stream and listening for new tweets.

Luckily, we don't need to implement this functionality ourselves because we can reuse another Snapkite module called `snapkite-stream-client`. Let's install this module:

1. Navigate to the `~/snapterest` directory and run the following command:

    npm install --save snapkite-stream-client

2. This will install the `snapkite-stream-client` module, and add it to `package.json` as a dependency.

3. Now we're ready to reuse the `snapkite-stream-client` module in one of our React components.

In the previous chapter, we created the `Application` component with two child components: `Stream` and `Collection`. In this chapter, we'll create our `Stream` component.

Let's start by creating the `~/snapterest/source/components/Stream.js` file:

```
import React, { Component } from 'react';
import SnapkiteStreamClient from 'snapkite-stream-client';
import StreamTweet from './StreamTweet';
import Header from './Header.react';

class Stream extends Component {
  state = {
    tweet: null
  }

  componentDidMount() {
    SnapkiteStreamClient.initializeStream(this.handleNewTweet);
  }

  componentWillUnmount() {
    SnapkiteStreamClient.destroyStream();
  }

  handleNewTweet = (tweet) => {
    this.setState({
      tweet: tweet
    });
  }

  render() {
```

```
      const { tweet } = this.state;
      const { onAddTweetToCollection } = this.props;
      const headerText = 'Waiting for public photos from Twitter...';

      if (tweet) {
        return (
          <StreamTweet
            tweet={tweet}
              onAddTweetToCollection={onAddTweetToCollection}
          />
        );
      }

      return (
        <Header text={headerText}/>
      );
    }
  }

  export default Stream;
```

First, we will import the following modules that our `Stream` component depends on:

- `React` and `ReactDOM`: This is part of the React library
- `StreamTweet` and `Header`: These are React components
- `snapkite-stream-client`: This is a ut   ility library

Then, we will define our React component. Let's take a look at the methods that our `Stream` component implements:

- `componentDidMount()`
- `componentWillUnmount()`
- `handleNewTweet()`
- `render()`

We're already familiar with the `render()` method. The `render()` method is part of React's API. You already know that any React component must implement at least the `render()` method. Let's take a look at the `render()` method of our `Stream` component:

```
render() {
  const { tweet } = this.state;
  const { onAddTweetToCollection } = this.props;
```

```
const headerText = 'Waiting for public photos from Twitter...';

if (tweet) {
  return (
    <StreamTweet
      tweet={tweet}
      onAddTweetToCollection={onAddTweetToCollection}
    />
  );
}

return (
  <Header text={headerText}/>
);
}
```

As you can see, we created a new `tweet` constant that references the `tweet` property, which is part of a component's state object. We will then check whether that variable has a reference to an actual `tweet` object, and if it does, our `render()` method returns the `StreamTweet` component, or else, it returns the `Header` component.

The `StreamTweet` component renders a header and the latest tweet from a stream, whereas the `Header` component renders only a header.

Have you noticed that our `Stream` component doesn't render anything itself, but rather returns one of the two other components that do the actual rendering? The purpose of a `Stream` component is to encapsulate our application's logic and delegate rendering to the other React components. In React, you should have at least one component that encapsulates your application's logic, and stores and manages your application's state. This is usually a root component or one of the high-level components in your component hierarchy. All the other child React components should have no state, if possible. If you think of all the React components as `Views`, then our `Stream` component is a `ControllerView` component.

Our `Stream` component will receive an endless stream of new tweets, and it needs to re-render its child components every time a new tweet is received. In order to achieve this, we need to store the current tweet in the component's state. Once we update its state, React will call its `render()` method and re-render all of its child components. For this purpose, we will implement the `handleNewTweet()` method:

```
handleNewTweet - (tweet) => {
  this.setState({
    tweet: tweet
  });
}
```

The `handleNewTweet()` method takes a `tweet` object, and sets it as a new value for the component state's `tweet` property.

Where does that new tweet come from and when does it come? Let's take a look at our `componentDidMount()` method:

```
componentDidMount() {
    SnapkiteStreamClient.initializeStream(this.handleNewTweet);
}
```

This method calls the `initializeStream()` property of the `SnapkiteStreamClient` object, and passes a `this.handleNewTweet` callback function as its argument. `SnapkiteStreamClient` is an external library with an API that we're using to initialize a stream of tweets. The `this.handleNewTweet` method will be called for every new tweet that `SnapkiteStreamClient` receives.

Why did we name this method `componentDidMount()`? We didn't. React did. In fact, the `componentDidMount()` method is part of React's API. It's one of the React component's lifecycle methods. It's called only once, immediately after React has finished the initial rendering of our component. At this point, React has created a DOM tree, which is represented by our component, and now we can access that DOM with another JavaScript library.

The `componentDidMount()` library is a perfect place for integrating React with another JavaScript library. This is where we connect to a stream of tweets using the external `SnapkiteStreamClient` library.

Now we know when to initialize the external JavaScript libraries in our React components, but what about the reverse process—when should we uninitialize and clean up everything that we've done in the `componentDidMount()` method? It's a good idea to clean up everything before we unmount our components. For this purpose, React API offers us another component lifecycle method—`componentWillUnmount()`:

```
componentWillUnmount() {
    SnapkiteStreamClient.destroyStream();
}
```

The `componentWillUnmount()` method is called by React just before React unmounts the component. As you can see in the `componentWillUnmount()` method, you're calling the `destroyStream()` property of the `SnapkiteStreamClient` object. The `destroyStream()` property cleans up our connection to `SnapkiteStreamClient`, and we can safely unmount our `Stream` component.

You might be wondering what the component lifecycle methods are, and why we need them.

Understanding React component's lifecycle methods

Think about what a React component does? It describes what to render. We know that it uses the render() method for this. However, sometimes, having only the render() method is not enough because what if we want to do something before or after the component has rendered? What if we want to be able to decide whether a component's render() method should be called at all?

Looks like what we're describing is a process during which the React component is rendered. This process has various stages, for example, before render, render, and after render. In React, this process is called the **component's lifecycle**. Each React component goes through this process. What we want is a way to hook into that process, and call our own functions at different stages of that process in order to have a greater control over it. For this purpose, React provides a number of methods that we can use to get notified when a certain stage in a component's lifecycle process occurs. These methods are called the **component's lifecycle methods**. They are called in a predictable order.

All the React component's lifecycle methods can be grouped into three phases:

- **Mounting**: This phase occurs when a component is being inserted into the DOM

- **Updating**: This phase occurs when a component is being re-rendered into a virtual DOM to figure out if the actual DOM needs to be updated

- **Unmounting**: This phase occurs when a component is being removed from the DOM:

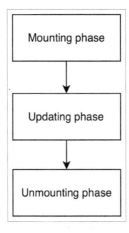

In React's terminology, inserting a component into the DOM is called "mounting," whereas removing a component from the DOM is called "unmounting."

The best way to learn about the React component's lifecycle methods is to see them in action. Let's create our `StreamTweet` component that we discussed earlier in this chapter. This component will implement most of React's lifecycle methods.

Navigate to `~/snapterest/source/components/` and create the `StreamTweet.js` file:

```
import React, { Component } from 'react';
import Header from './Header';
import Tweet from './Tweet';

class StreamTweet extends Component {

  // define other component lifecycle methods here

  render() {
    console.log('[Snapterest] StreamTweet: Running render()');

    const { headerText } = this.state;
    const { tweet, onAddTweetToCollection } = this.props;

    return (
      <section>
        <Header text={headerText} />
        <Tweet
          tweet={tweet}
          onImageClick={onAddTweetToCollection}
        />
      </section>
    );
  }
}

export default StreamTweet;
```

As you can see, the `StreamTweet` component has no lifecycle methods yet, other than `render()`. We'll create and discuss them one by one as we move ahead.

The four methods are called during a component's *mounting* phase, as shown in the following figure:

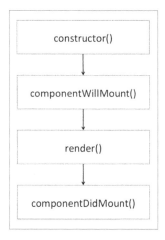

As you can see from the preceding figure, the methods called are as follows:

- constructor()
- componentWillMount()
- render()
- componentDidMount()

In this chapter, we'll discuss two of these four methods (except render()). They are called only once when the component is inserted into the DOM. Let's take a closer look at each of them.

Mounting methods

Now let's look at some of the useful mounting methods.

The componentWillMount method

The componentWillMount() method is invoked second. It is invoked *immediately before* React inserts a component into the DOM. Add this code right after the constructor() method in your StreamTweet component:

```
componentWillMount() {
    console.log('[Snapterest] StreamTweet: 1. Running
    componentWillMount()');

    this.setState({
```

```
    numberOfCharactersIsIncreasing: true,
    headerText: 'Latest public photo from Twitter'
  });

  window.snapterest = {
    numberOfReceivedTweets: 1,
    numberOfDisplayedTweets: 1
  };
}
```

We do a number of things in this method. First, we log the fact that this method is being invoked. In fact, for the purpose of demonstration, we'll log every component lifecycle method of this component. When you run this code in a web browser, you should be able to open the JavaScript console, and see these log messages printed in the expected ascending order.

Next, we update the component's state using the `this.setState()` method:

- Set the `numberOfCharactersIsIncreasing` property to `true`
- Set the `headerText` property to `'Latest public photo from Twitter'`

Because this is the very first tweet that this component will render, we know that the number of characters is definitely increasing from nothing to the number of characters in that first tweet. Hence, we set it to `true`. We also assign the default text to our header, `'Latest public photo from Twitter'`.

As you know, calling the `this.setState()` method should trigger the component's `render()` method, so it seems like `render()` will be called twice during the component's mounting phase. However, in this case, React knows that nothing has been rendered yet, so it will call the `render()` method only once.

Finally, in this method, we define a `snapterest` global object with the following two properties:

- `numberOfReceivedTweets`: This property counts the number of all the received tweets
- `numberOfDisplayedTweets`: This property counts the number of only the displayed tweets

We set `numberOfReceivedTweets` to 1 because we know that the `componentWillMount()` method is called only once when the very first tweet is received. We also know that our `render()` method will be called for this very first tweet, so we set `numberOfDisplayedTweets` to 1 as well:

```
window.snapterest = {
  numberOfReceivedTweets: 1,
  numberOfDisplayedTweets: 1
};
```

This global object is not part of React or our web application's logic; we can remove it and everything will still work as expected. In the preceding code, `window.snapterest` is a convenience tool used to keep track of how many tweets we've processed at any point in time. We use the global `window.snapterest` object for demonstration purposes only. I would strongly advise you against adding your own properties to a global object in real-life projects because you might overwrite the existing properties, and/or your properties might be overwritten later by some other JavaScript code that you don't own. Later on, if you decide to deploy Snapterest in production, then make sure to remove the global `window.snapterest` object and the related code from the `StreamTweet` component.

After viewing Snapterest in a web browser for a few minutes, you can open the JavaScript console and type the `snapterest.numberOfReceivedTweets` and `snapterest.numberOfDisplayedTweets` commands. These commands will output the numbers that will help you get a better understanding of how fast the new tweets are coming, and how many of them are not being displayed. In our next component lifecycle method, we'll add more properties to our `window.snapterest` object.

The componentDidMount method

The `componentDidMount()` method is invoked *immediately after* React inserts a component into the DOM. The updated DOM is now available for access, which means that this method is the best place for initializing other JavaScript libraries that need access to that DOM.

Earlier in this chapter, we created our `Stream` component with the `componentDidMount()` method that initializes the external `snapkite-stream-client` JavaScript library.

Let's take a look at this component's `componentDidMount()` method. Add the following code to your `StreamTweet` component after the `componentWillMount()` method:

```
componentDidMount = () => {
  console.log('[Snapterest] StreamTweet: 3. Running
componentDidMount()');

  const componentDOMRepresentation = ReactDOM.findDOMNode(this);

  window.snapterest.headerHtml =
  componentDOMRepresentation.children[0].outerHTML;
  window.snapterest.tweetHtml =
  componentDOMRepresentation.children[1].outerHTML;
}
```

Here, we're referencing the DOM that represents our `StreamTweet` component using the `ReactDOM.findDOMNode()` method. We pass `this` parameter that references the current component (in this case, `StreamTweet`). The `componentDOMRepresentation` constant references the DOM tree that we can traverse and, thereby, access its various properties. To get a good understanding of what this DOM tree looks like, let's take a closer look at the `render()` method of our `StreamTweet` component:

```
render() {
  console.log('[Snapterest] StreamTweet: Running render()');

  const { headerText } = this.state;
  const { tweet, onAddTweetToCollection } = this.props;

  return (
    <section>
      <Header text={headerText} />
      <Tweet
        tweet={tweet}
        onImageClick={onAddTweetToCollection}
      />
    </section>
  );
}
```

One of the greatest benefits of using JSX is that we can easily identify how many child elements our component will have just by looking at the component's `render()` method. Here, we can see that a parent `<section>` element has two child components: `<Header/>` and `<Tweet/>`.

So when we traverse the resulting DOM tree using the DOM API `children` property, we can be sure that it will have two child elements as well:

- `componentDOMRepresentation.children[0]`: This is our `<Header />` component's DOM representation
- `componentDOMRepresentation.children[1]`: This is our `<Tweet />` component's DOM representation

The `outerHTML` attribute of each element gets the HTML string that represents the DOM tree of each element. We assign this HTML string to our global `window.snapterest` object for convenience, as we discussed earlier in this chapter.

If you are using another JavaScript library, such as **jQuery**, along with React, then use the `componentDidMount()` method as an opportunity to integrate the two. If you want to send an AJAX request, or set timers using the `setTimeout()` or `setInterval()` functions, then you can do that in this method as well. In general, `componentDidMount()` should be your preferred component lifecycle method for integrating the React library with nonReact libraries and APIs.

So far, in this chapter, you've learned the fundamental mounting methods that the React component provides us with. We used all three of them in our `StreamTweet` component. We also discussed the `StreamTweet` component's `render()` method. This is all that we need to know to understand how React will render the `StreamTweet` component initially. On its very first render, React will execute the following sequence of methods:

- `componentWillMount()`
- `render()`
- `componentDidMount()`

This is called the React component's **mounting phase**. It's executed only once, unless we unmount a component and mount it again.

Next, let's discuss the React component's **unmounting phase**.

Unmounting methods

Let's now take a look at one of the popular unmounting methods.

The componentWillUnmount method

React offers only one method for this phase, that is, componentWillUnmount().
It is invoked *immediately before* React removes a component from the DOM and
destroys it. This method is useful for cleaning up any data that is created during
the component's mounting or updating phases. This is exactly what we do in our
StreamTweet component. Add this code to your StreamTweet component after the
componentDidMount() method:

```
componentWillUnmount() {
  console.log('[Snapterest] StreamTweet: 8. Running
  componentWillUnmount()');

  delete window.snapterest;
}
```

In the componentWillUnmount() method, we delete our global window.snapterest
object using the delete operator:

```
delete window.snapterest;
```

Removing window.snapterest will keep our global object clean. If you've created
any additional DOM elements in the componentDidMount() method, then the
componentWillUnmount() method is a good place to remove them. You can think
of the componentDidMount() and componentWillUnmount() methods as a two-step
mechanism for integrating the React component with another JavaScript API:

1. Initialize it in the componentDidMount() method.
2. Terminate it in the componentWillUnmount() method.

In this way, your external JavaScript libraries that need to work with the DOM will
stay in sync with the DOM rendered by React.

That's all we need to know to efficiently unmount React components.

Summary

In this chapter, we created our `Stream` component and learned how to integrate a React component with the external JavaScript library. You also learned about the React component's lifecycle methods. We also focused on and discussed the mounting and unmounting methods in detail and started implementing the `StreamTweet` component.

In our next chapter, we'll take a look at the component lifecycle's updating methods. We'll also implement our `Header` and `Tweet` components, and learn how to set the component's default properties.

7
Updating Your React Components

In the previous chapter, you learned that a React component can go through three phases:

- Mounting
- Updating
- Unmounting

We've already discussed the mounting and unmounting phases. In this chapter, we'll focus on the updating phase. During this phase, a React component is already inserted into the DOM. This DOM represents a component's current state, and when that state changes, React needs to evaluate how a new state is going to mutate the previously rendered DOM.

React provides us with methods to influence what is going to be rendered during an update as well as to be aware of when an update happens. These methods allow us to control the transition from the current component's state to the next component's state. Let's learn more about the powerful nature of the React component's updating methods.

Understanding component lifecycle updating methods

A React component has five lifecycle methods that belong to a component's *updating* phase:

- `componentWillReceiveProps()`
- `shouldComponentUpdate()`

- componentWillUpdate()
- render()
- componentDidUpdate()

See the following figure for a better view:

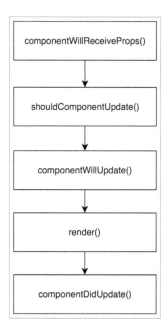

You're already familiar with the render() method. Now let's discuss the other four methods.

The componentWillReceiveProps method

We'll start with the componentWillReceiveProps() method in the StreamTweet component. Add the following code after the componentDidMount() method in the StreamTweet.js file:

```
componentWillReceiveProps(nextProps) {
  console.log('[Snapterest] StreamTweet: 4. Running
  componentWillReceiveProps()');

  const { tweet: currentTweet } = this.props;
  const { tweet: nextTweet } = nextProps;

  const currentTweetLength = currentTweet.text.length;
  const nextTweetLength = nextTweet.text.length;
```

```
    const isNumberOfCharactersIncreasing = (nextTweetLength >
    currentTweetLength);
    let headerText;

    this.setState({
      numberOfCharactersIsIncreasing: isNumberOfCharactersIncreasing
    });

    if (isNumberOfCharactersIncreasing) {
      headerText = 'Number of characters is increasing';
    } else {
      headerText = 'Latest public photo from Twitter';
    }

    this.setState({
      headerText
    });

    window.snapterest.numberOfReceivedTweets++;
}
```

This method is invoked first in the component lifecycle's updating phase. It is called when a component receives new properties from its parent component.

This method is an opportunity for us to compare the current component's properties, using the `this.props` object, with the next component's properties, using the `nextProps` object. Based on this comparison, we can choose to update the component's state using the `this.setState()` function, which will not trigger an additional render in this scenario.

Let's see that in action:

```
const { tweet: currentTweet } = this.props;
const { tweet: nextTweet } = nextProps;

const currentTweetLength = currentTweet.text.length;
const nextTweetLength = nextTweet.text.length;
const isNumberOfCharactersIncreasing = (nextTweetLength >
currentTweetLength);
let headerText;

this.setState({
  numberOfCharactersIsIncreasing: isNumberOfCharactersIncreasing
});
```

We first get the lengths of the current tweet and the next tweet. The current one is available via `this.props.tweet` and the next one via `nextProps.tweet`. We then compare their lengths by checking whether the next tweet is longer than the current one. The result of the comparison is stored in the `isNumberOfCharactersIncreasing` variable. Finally, we update the component's state by setting the `numberOfCharactersIsIncreasing` property to the value of our `isNumberOfCharactersIncreasing` variable.

We then set our header text as follows:

```
if (isNumberOfCharactersIncreasing) {
  headerText = 'Number of characters is increasing';
} else {
  headerText = 'Latest public photo from Twitter';
}

this.setState({
  headerText
});
```

If the next tweet is longer, we set the header text to `'Number of characters is increasing'`, or else, we set it to `'Latest public photo from Twitter'`. We then update our component's state once more by setting the `headerText` property to the value of our `headerText` variable.

Notice that we call the `this.setState()` function twice in our `componentWillReceiveProps()` method. This is to illustrate the point that no matter how many times you call `this.setState()` in the `componentWillReceiveProps()` method, it won't trigger any additional renders of that component. React does an internal optimization, where it batches the state updates together.

Since the `componentWillReceiveProps()` method will be called once for each new tweet that our `StreamTweet` component will receive, it makes it a good place to count the total number of received tweets:

```
window.snapterest.numberOfReceivedTweets++;
```

Now we know how to check whether the next tweet is longer than the tweet we're currently displaying, but how can we choose not to render the next tweet at all?

The shouldComponentUpdate method

The `shouldComponentUpdate()` method allows us to decide whether the next component's state should trigger the component's re-rendering or not. This method returns a Boolean value, which by default is `true`, but you can return `false`, and the following component methods won't be called:

- `componentWillUpdate()`
- `render()`
- `componentDidUpdate()`

Skipping a call to the component's `render()` method will prevent that component from re-rendering, which in turn will improve your application's performance, since no additional DOM mutations will be made.

This method is invoked second in the component lifecycle's updating phase.

This method is a great place for us to prevent the next tweet with one or less characters from being displayed. Add this code to the `StreamTweet` component after the `componentWillReceiveProps()` method:

```
shouldComponentUpdate(nextProps, nextState) {
  console.log('[Snapterest] StreamTweet: 5. Running
  shouldComponentUpdate()');

  return (nextProps.tweet.text.length > 1);
}
```

If the next tweet's length is greater than 1, then `shouldComponentUpdate()` returns `true`, and the `StreamTweet` component renders the next tweet. Or else, it returns `false`, and the `StreamTweet` component doesn't render the next state.

The componentWillUpdate method

The `componentWillUpdate()` method is called *immediately before* React updates the DOM. It gets the following two arguments:

- `nextProps`: The next properties object
- `nextState`: The next state object

You can use these arguments to prepare for the DOM update. However, you cannot use `this.setState()` in the `componentWillUpdate()` method. If you want to update the component's state in response to its properties changing, then do that in the `componentWillReceiveProps()` method, which will be called by React when the properties change.

To demonstrate when the `componentWillUpdate()` method is called, we need to log it in the `StreamTweet` component. Add this code after the `shouldComponentUpdate()` method:

```
componentWillUpdate(nextProps, nextState) {
  console.log('[Snapterest] StreamTweet: 6. Running
  componentWillUpdate()');
}
```

After calling the `componentWillUpdate()` method, React invokes the `render()` method that performs the DOM update. Then, the `componentDidUpdate()` method is called.

The componentDidUpdate method

The `componentDidUpdate()` method is called *immediately after* React updates the DOM. It gets these two arguments:

- `prevProps`: The previous properties object
- `prevState`: The previous state object

We will use this method to interact with the updated DOM or perform any post-render operations. In our `StreamTweet` component, we'll use `componentDidUpdate()` to increment the number of displayed tweets in our global object. Add this code after the `componentWillUpdate()` method:

```
componentDidUpdate(prevProps, prevState) {
  console.log('[Snapterest] StreamTweet: 7. Running
  componentDidUpdate()');

  window.snapterest.numberOfDisplayedTweets++;
}
```

After `componentDidUpdate()` is called, the updating cycle ends. A new cycle is started when a component's state is updated or a parent component passes new properties. Or when you call the `forceUpdate()` method, it triggers a new updating cycle, but skips the `shouldComponentUpdate()` method on a component that triggered the update. However, `shouldComponentUpdate()` is called on all child components as per the usual updating phase. Try to avoid using the `forceUpdate()` method as much as possible; this will promote your application's maintainability.

This concludes our discussion of React component lifecycle methods.

Setting default React component properties

As you know from the previous chapter, our `StreamTweet` component renders two child components: `Header` and `Tweet`.

Let's create these components. To do this, navigate to `~/snapterest/source/components/` and create the `Header.js` file:

```
import React from 'react';

export const DEFAULT_HEADER_TEXT = 'Default header';

const headerStyle = {
  fontSize: '16px',
  fontWeight: '300',
  display: 'inline-block',
  margin: '20px 10px'
};

class Header extends React.Component {

  render() {
    const { text } = this.props;

    return (
      <h2 style={headerStyle}>{text}</h2>
    );
  }
}

Header.defaultProps = {
  text: DEFAULT_HEADER_TEXT
};

export default Header;
```

As you can see, our `Header` component is a stateless component that renders the `h2` element. The header text is passed from a parent component as a `this.props.text` property, which makes this component flexible, that allows us to reuse it anywhere where we need a header. We'll reuse this component again later in this book.

Notice that the h2 element has a style property.

In React, we can define the CSS rules in a JavaScript object, and then pass that object as a value to the React element's style property. For example, in this component, we define the headerStyle variable that references an object where:

- Each object key is a CSS property
- Each object value is a CSS value

The CSS properties that contain a hyphen in their names should be converted to the **camelCase** style; for example, font-size becomes fontSize and font-weight becomes fontWeight.

The advantages of defining your CSS rules inside a React component are as follows:

- **Portability**: You can easily share a component together with its styling, all in one JavaScript file
- **Encapsulation**: Making styles inline allows you to limit the scope of what they affect
- **Flexibility**: The CSS rules can be calculated using the power of JavaScript

The significant disadvantage of using this technique is the fact that **Content Security Policies (CSP)** can block inline styling from having any effect. You can learn more about CSP at https://developer.mozilla.org/en-US/docs/Web/HTTP/CSP.

Our Header component has one property that we haven't discussed yet, that is, defaultProps. What if you forget to pass a property that a React component depends on? In that case, a component can set the default properties using the defaultProps property; consider the following example:

```
Header.defaultProps = {
  text: DEFAULT_HEADER_TEXT
};
```

In this example, we're setting a default value of 'Default header' to our text property. If a parent component passes the this.props.text property, then it will overwrite the default one.

Next, let's create our Tweet component. To do this, navigate to ~/snapterest/ source/components/ and create the Tweet.js file:

```
import React from 'react';
import PropTypes from 'prop-types';

const tweetStyle = {
  position: 'relative',
```

```
      display: 'inline-block',
      width: '300px',
      height: '400px',
      margin: '10px'
};

const imageStyle = {
    maxHeight: '400px',
    maxWidth: '100%',
    boxShadow: '0px 1px 1px 0px #aaa',
    border: '1px solid #fff'
};

class Tweet extends React.Component {
    handleImageClick() {
        const { tweet, onImageClick } = this.props;

        if (onImageClick) {
            onImageClick(tweet);
        }
    }

    render() {
        const { tweet } = this.props;
        const tweetMediaUrl = tweet.media[0].url;

        return (
            <div style={tweetStyle}>
                <img
                    src={tweetMediaUrl}
                    onClick={this.handleImageClick}
                    style={imageStyle}
                />
            </div>
        );
    }
}

Tweet.propTypes = {
    tweet: (properties, propertyName, componentName) => {
        const tweet = properties[propertyName];

        if (! tweet) {
            return new Error('Tweet must be set.');
```

```
    }

    if (! tweet.media) {
      return new Error('Tweet must have an image.');
    }
  },
  onImageClick: PropTypes.func
};

export default Tweet;
```

This component renders a `<div>` element with a child `<img>` element. Both the elements have inline styles, and the `<img>` element has a click event handler, that is, `this.handleImageClick`:

```
handleImageClick() {
  const { tweet, onImageClick } = this.props;

  if (onImageClick) {
    onImageClick(tweet);
  }
}
```

When a user clicks on a tweet's image, the `Tweet` component checks whether a parent component has passed a `this.props.onImageClick` callback function as a property and calls that function. The `this.props.onImageClick` property is an optional `Tweet` component's property, so we need to check whether it was passed before we can use it. On the other hand, `tweet` is a required property.

How can we ensure that a component receives all the required properties?

Validating React component properties

In React, there is a way to validate the component properties using the component's `propTypes` object:

```
Component.propTypes = {
  propertyName: validator
};
```

In this object, you need to specify a property name and a validator function that will determine whether a property is valid or not. React provides some predefined validators for you to reuse. They are all available in the `PropTypes` object from the `prop-types` package:

- `PropTypes.number`: This will validate whether a property is a number or not
- `PropTypes.string`: This will validate whether a property is a string or not
- `PropTypes.bool`: This will validate whether a property is a Boolean or not
- `PropTypes.object`: This will validate whether a property is an object or not
- `PropTypes.element`: This will validate whether a property is a React element or not

For a complete list of the `PropTypes` validators, you can check the docs at `https://facebook.github.io/react/docs/typechecking-with-proptypes.html`.

By default, all the properties that you validate with the `PropTypes` validators are optional. You can chain any of them with `isRequired` to make sure that a warning message is displayed on a JavaScript console when a property is missing:

```
Component.propTypes = {
  propertyName: PropTypes.number.isRequired
};
```

You can also specify your own custom validator function that should return an `Error` object if the validation fails:

```
Component.propTypes = {
  propertyName(properties, propertyName, componentName) {
    // ... validation failed
    return new Error('A property is not valid.');
  }
};
```

Let's take a look at the `propTypes` object in our `Tweet` component:

```
Tweet.propTypes = {
  tweet(properties, propertyName, componentName) {
    const tweet = properties[propertyName];

    if (!tweet) {
      return new Error('Tweet must be set.');
    }

    if (!tweet.media) {
```

```
        return new Error('Tweet must have an image.');
      }
    },
    onImageClick: PropTypes.func
  };
```

As you can see, we're validating two `Tweet` component properties: `tweet` and `onImageClick`.

We use the custom validator function to validate the `tweet` property. React passes three parameters to this function:

- `properties`: This is the component properties object
- `propertyName`: This is the name of the property that we're validating
- `componentName`: This is the name of the component

We first check whether our `Tweet` component received the `tweet` property:

```
const tweet = properties[propertyName];

if (!tweet) {
  return new Error('Tweet must be set.');
}
```

Then, we assume that the `tweet` property is an object, and check whether that object has no `media` property:

```
if (!tweet.media) {
  return new Error('Tweet must have an image.');
}
```

Both of these checks return an `Error` object that will be logged in a JavaScript console.

Another `Tweet` component's property that we will validate is `onImageClick`:

```
onImageClick: PropTypes.func
```

We validate that the value of the `onImageClick` property is a function. In this case, we reuse a validator function provided by the `PropTypes` object. As you can see, `onImageClick` is an optional property because we didn't add `isRequired`.

Finally, for performance reasons, `propTypes` is only checked in the development version of React.

Creating a Collection component

You might recall that our topmost hierarchy `Application` component has two child components: `Stream` and `Collection`.

So far, we've discussed and implemented our `Stream` component and its child components. Next, we're going to focus on our `Collection` component.

Create the `~/snapterest/source/components/Collection.js` file:

```
import React, { Component } from 'react';
import ReactDOMServer from 'react-dom/server';
import CollectionControls from './CollectionControls';
import TweetList from './TweetList';
import Header from './Header';

class Collection extends Component {
  createHtmlMarkupStringOfTweetList = () => {
    const { tweets } = this.props;

    const htmlString = ReactDOMServer.renderToStaticMarkup(
      <TweetList tweets={tweets} />
    );

    const htmlMarkup = {
      html: htmlString
    };

    return JSON.stringify(htmlMarkup);
  }

  getListOfTweetIds = () =>
    Object.keys(this.props.tweets)

  getNumberOfTweetsInCollection = () =>
    this.getListOfTweetIds().length

  render() {
    const numberOfTweetsInCollection =
    this.getNumberOfTweetsInCollection();

    if (numberOfTweetsInCollection > 0) {
      const {
        tweets,
```

```
          onRemoveAllTweetsFromCollection,
          onRemoveTweetFromCollection
        } = this.props;

      const htmlMarkup = this.createHtmlMarkupStringOfTweetList();

      return (
        <div>
          <CollectionControls
            numberOfTweetsInCollection=
            {numberOfTweetsInCollection}
            htmlMarkup={htmlMarkup}
            onRemoveAllTweetsFromCollection=
            {onRemoveAllTweetsFromCollection}
          />

          <TweetList
            tweets={tweets}
            onRemoveTweetFromCollection=
            {onRemoveTweetFromCollection}
          />

        </div>
      );
    }

    return <Header text="Your collection is empty"/>;
  }
}

export default Collection;
```

Our `Collection` component is responsible for rendering two things:

- Tweets that the user has collected
- User interface control elements for manipulating that collection

Let's take a look at the component's `render()` method:

```
render() {
  const numberOfTweetsInCollection =
  this.getNumberOfTweetsInCollection();

  if (numberOfTweetsInCollection > 0) {
    const {
```

```
      tweets,
      onRemoveAllTweetsFromCollection,
      onRemoveTweetFromCollection
    } = this.props;

    const htmlMarkup = this.createHtmlMarkupStringOfTweetList();

    return (
      <div>
        <CollectionControls
          numberOfTweetsInCollection={numberOfTweetsInCollection}
          htmlMarkup={htmlMarkup}
          onRemoveAllTweetsFromCollection=
          {onRemoveAllTweetsFromCollection}
        />

        <TweetList
          tweets={tweets}
          onRemoveTweetFromCollection=
          {onRemoveTweetFromCollection}
        />

      </div>
    );
  }

  return <Header text="Your collection is empty"/>;
}
```

We first get a number of tweets in the collection using the `this.getNumberOfTweetsInCollection()` method:

```
getNumberOfTweetsInCollection = () =>
  this.getListOfTweetIds().length
```

This method, in turn, uses another method to get a list of tweet IDs:

```
getListOfTweetIds = () => Object.keys(this.props.tweets);
```

The `this.getListOfTweetIds()` function call returns an array of tweet IDs, and then `this.getNumberOfTweetsInCollection()` returns a length of that array.

In our `render()` method, once we know the number of tweets in our collection, we have to make a choice:

- If the collection is *not* empty, then render the `CollectionControls` and `TweetList` components
- Otherwise, render the `Header` component

What do all these components render?

- The `CollectionControls` component renders a header with a collection name and a set of buttons that allow users to rename, empty, and export a collection
- The `TweetList` component renders a list of tweets
- The `Header` component simply renders a header with a message that the collection is empty

The idea is to only show a collection when it's not empty. In that case, we're creating four variables:

```
const {
  tweets,
  onRemoveAllTweetsFromCollection,
  onRemoveTweetFromCollection
} = this.props;

const htmlMarkup = this.createHtmlMarkupStringOfTweetList();
```

- The `tweets` variable references our `tweets` property that is passed from a parent component
- The `htmlMarkup` variable references a string that is returned by the component's `this.createHtmlMarkupStringOfTweetList()` function call
- The `onRemoveAllTweetsFromCollection` and `onRemoveTweetFromCollection` variables reference functions that are passed from a parent component

As the name suggests, the `this.createHtmlMarkupStringOfTweetList()` method creates a string that represents the HTML markup created by rendering the `TweetList` component:

```
createHtmlMarkupStringOfTweetList = () => {
  const { tweets } = this.props;

  const htmlString = ReactDOMServer.renderToStaticMarkup(
    <TweetList tweets={tweets}/>
```

```
  );

  const htmlMarkup = {
    html: htmlString
  };

  return JSON.stringify(htmlMarkup);
}
```

The `createHtmlMarkupStringOfTweetList()` method uses the `ReactDOMServer.renderToStaticMarkup()` function that we discussed in *Chapter 3, Creating Your First React Element*. We pass the `TweetList` component as its argument:

```
const htmlString = ReactDOMServer.renderToStaticMarkup(
  <TweetList tweets={tweets} />
);
```

This `TweetList` component has a `tweets` property that references the `tweets` property passed by a parent component.

The resulting HTML string produced by the `ReactDOMServer.renderToStaticMarkup()` function is stored in the `htmlString` variable. Then, we create a new `htmlMarkup` object with the `html` property that references our `htmlString` variable. Finally, we use the `JSON.stringify()` function to convert our `htmlMarkup` JavaScript object to a JSON string. The result of the `JSON.stringify(htmlMarkup)` function call is what our `createHtmlMarkupStringOfTweetList()` method returns.

This method demonstrates how flexible React components are; you can use the same React components to render the DOM elements as well as produce a string of HTML markup that can be passed to a third-party API.

Another interesting observation that one can make is the use of JSX syntax outside a `render()` method. In fact, you can use JSX anywhere in your source file, even outside of component class declarations.

Let's take a closer look at what the `Collection` component returns when our collection is *not* empty:

```
return (
  <div>
    <CollectionControls
      numberOfTweetsInCollection={numberOfTweetsInCollection}
      htmlMarkup={htmlMarkup}
      onRemoveAllTweetsFromCollection=
      {onRemoveAllTweetsFromCollection}
```

```
      />

    <TweetList
      tweets={tweets}
      onRemoveTweetFromCollection={onRemoveTweetFromCollection}
      />

  </div>
);
```

We wrap the `CollectionControls` and `TweetList` components in the `<div>` element because React allows only one root element. Let's take a look at each component and discuss its properties.

We pass the following three properties to the `CollectionControls` component:

- The `numberOfTweetsInCollection` property references the current number of tweets in our collection.

- The `htmlMarkup` property references a string of HTML markup that we produce in this component using the `createHtmlMarkupStringOfTweetList()` method.

- The `onRemoveAllTweetsFromCollection` property references a function that removes all the tweets from our collection. This function is implemented in the `Application` component and discussed in *Chapter 5, Making Your React Components Reactive*.

We pass these two properties to the `TweetList` component:

- The `tweets` property references tweets passed from a parent `Application` component.

- The `onRemoveTweetFromCollection` property references a function that removes a tweet from a collection of tweets that we store in the `Application` component's state. We have already discussed this function in *Chapter 5, Making Your React Components Reactive*.

And that's our `Collection` component.

Summary

In this chapter, you learned about the updating methods of the lifecycle of a component. We also discussed how to validate the component properties and set default property values. We also made good progress with our Snapterest application; we created and discussed the `Header`, `Tweet`, and `Collection` components.

In the next chapter, we'll focus on building more complex React components and finish building our Snapterest application!

8
Building Complex React Components

In this chapter, we'll put everything you learned so far about React components in action by building the most complex components in our application, that is, the child components of our `Collection` component. Our aim in this chapter is to gain solid React experience and grow our React muscle. Let's get started!

Creating the TweetList component

As you know, our `Collection` component has two child components: `CollectionControls` and `TweetList`.

We'll first build the `TweetList` component. Create the following `~/snapterest/source/components/TweetList.js` file:

```
import React, { Component } from 'react';
import Tweet from './Tweet';
import TweetUtils from '../utils/TweetUtils';

const listStyle = {
  padding: '0'
};

const listItemStyle = {
  display: 'inline-block',
  listStyle: 'none'
};

class TweetList extends Component {
```

```
    getTweetElement = (tweetId) => {
      const { tweets, onRemoveTweetFromCollection } = this.props;
      const tweet = tweets[tweetId];
      let tweetElement;

      if (onRemoveTweetFromCollection) {
        tweetElement = (
          <Tweet
            tweet={tweet}
            onImageClick={onRemoveTweetFromCollection}
          />
        );
      } else {
        tweetElement = <Tweet tweet={tweet}/>;
      }

      return (
        <li style={listItemStyle} key={tweet.id}>
          {tweetElement}
        </li>
      );
    }

    render() {
      const tweetElements = TweetUtils
        .getListOfTweetIds()
        .map(this.getTweetElement);

      return (
        <ul style={listStyle}>
          {tweetElements}
        </ul>
      );
    }
  }

  export default TweetList;
```

The `TweetList` component renders a list of tweets:

```
  render() {
    const tweetElements = TweetUtils
      .getListOfTweetIds()
```

```
    .map(this.getTweetElement);

  return (
    <ul style={listStyle}>
      {tweetElements}
    </ul>
  );
}
```

First, we create a list of `Tweet` elements:

```
const tweetElements = TweetUtils
  .getListOfTweetIds()
  .map(this.getTweetElement);
```

The `TweetUtils.getListOfTweetIds()` method returns an array of tweet IDs.

Then, for each tweet ID in that array, we create a `Tweet` component. For this, we will call the `map()` method on our array of tweet IDs and pass the `this.getTweetElement` method as an argument:

```
getTweetElement = (tweetId) => {
  const { tweets, onRemoveTweetFromCollection } = this.props;
  const tweet = tweets[tweetId];
  let tweetElement;

  if (onRemoveTweetFromCollection) {
    tweetElement = (
      <Tweet
        tweet={tweet}
        onImageClick={onRemoveTweetFromCollection}
      />
    );
  } else {
    tweetElement = <Tweet tweet={tweet} />;
  }

  return (
    <li style={listItemStyle} key={tweet.id}>
      {tweetElement}
    </li>
  );
}
```

The getTweetElement() method returns a Tweet element wrapped in the <li> element. As we already know, the Tweet component has an optional onImageClick property. When do we want to provide this optional property and when don't we?

There are two scenarios. In the first scenario, the user will click on a tweet image to remove it from a collection of tweets. In this scenario, our Tweet component will react to a click event, so we need to provide the onImageClick property. In the second scenario, the user will export a static collection of tweets that has no user interaction. In this scenario, we don't need to provide the onImageClick property.

This is exactly what we do in our getTweetElement() method:

```
const { tweets, onRemoveTweetFromCollection } = this.props;
const tweet = tweets[tweetId];
let tweetElement;

if (onRemoveTweetFromCollection) {
  tweetElement = (
    <Tweet
      tweet={tweet}
      onImageClick={onRemoveTweetFromCollection}
    />
  );
} else {
  tweetElement = <Tweet tweet={tweet}/>;
}
```

We create a tweet constant that stores a tweet with an ID that is provided by the tweetId argument. Then, we create a constant that stores the this.props. onRemoveTweetFromCollection property that is passed by a parent Collection component.

Next, we check whether the this.props.onRemoveTweetFromCollection property is provided by a Collection component. If it is, then we create a Tweet element with an onImageClick property:

```
tweetElement = (
  <Tweet
    tweet={tweet}
    onImageClick={onRemoveTweetFromCollection}
  />
);
```

If it isn't provided, then we create a `Tweet` element without a `handleImageClick` property:

```
tweetElement = <Tweet tweet={tweet} />;
```

We use the `TweetList` component in the following two cases:

- This component is used when rendering a collection of tweets in the `Collection` component. In this case, the `onRemoveTweetFromCollection` property *is* provided.
- This component is used when rendering a string of HTML markup that represents a collection of tweets in the `Collection` component. In this case, the `onRemoveTweetFromCollection` property *is not* provided.

Once we create our `Tweet` element, and put it into the `tweetElement` variable, we return the `<li>` element with an inline style:

```
return (
  <li style={listItemStyle} key={tweet.id}>
    {tweetElement}
  </li>
);
```

Besides the `style` property, our `<li>` element has a `key` property. It is used by React to identify each child element that is created dynamically. I recommend that you read more about Dynamic Children at `https://facebook.github.io/react/docs/lists-and-keys.html`.

This is how the `getTweetElement()` method works. As a result, the `TweetList` component returns an unordered list of `Tweet` elements:

```
return (
  <ul style={listStyle}>
    {tweetElements}
  </ul>
);
```

Creating the CollectionControls component

Now, since you understand what the `Collection` component renders, let's discuss its child components. We'll start with `CollectionControls`. Create the following `~/snapterest/source/components/CollectionControls.js` file:

```
import React, { Component } from 'react';
import Header from './Header';
import Button from './Button';
import CollectionRenameForm from './CollectionRenameForm';
import CollectionExportForm from './CollectionExportForm';

class CollectionControls extends Component {
  state = {
    name: 'new',
    isEditingName: false
  };

  getHeaderText = () => {
    const { name } = this.state;
    const { numberOfTweetsInCollection } = this.props;
    let text = numberOfTweetsInCollection;

    if (numberOfTweetsInCollection === 1) {
      text = `${text} tweet in your`;
    } else {
      text = `${text} tweets in your`;
    }

    return (
      <span>
        {text} <strong>{name}</strong> collection
      </span>
    );
  }

  toggleEditCollectionName = () => {
    this.setState(prevState => ({
      isEditingName: !prevState.isEditingName
    }));
  }

  setCollectionName = (name) => {
```

```
      this.setState({
        name,
        isEditingName: false
      });
    }

    render() {
      const { name, isEditingName } = this.state;
      const {
        onRemoveAllTweetsFromCollection,
        htmlMarkup
      } = this.props;

      if (isEditingName) {
        return (
          <CollectionRenameForm
            name={name}
            onChangeCollectionName={this.setCollectionName}
            onCancelCollectionNameChange=
            {this.toggleEditCollectionName}
          />
        );
      }

      return (
        <div>
          <Header text={this.getHeaderText()}/>

          <Button
            label="Rename collection"
            handleClick={this.toggleEditCollectionName}
          />

          <Button
            label="Empty collection"
            handleClick={onRemoveAllTweetsFromCollection}
          />

          <CollectionExportForm htmlMarkup={htmlMarkup} />
        </div>
      );
    }
}

export default CollectionControls;
```

The CollectionControls component, as the name suggests, renders a user interface to control a collection. These controls allow the user to do the following:

- Rename a collection
- Empty a collection
- Export a collection

A collection has a name. By default, this name is new and users can change it. A collection name is displayed in a header that is rendered by the CollectionControls component. This component is a perfect candidate for storing the collection's name, and since changing a name will require a component re-render, we'll store that name in the component's state object:

```
state = {
  name: 'new',
  isEditingName: false
};
```

The CollectionControls component can render either collection control elements or a form to change the collection name. A user can switch between the two. We need a way to represent these two states—we'll use the isEditingName property for that purpose. By default, isEditingName is set to false; therefore, users won't see a form to change the collection name, when the CollectionControls component is mounted. Let's take a look at its render() method:

```
render() {
  const { name, isEditingName } = this.state;
  const {
    onRemoveAllTweetsFromCollection,
    htmlMarkup
  } = this.props;

  if (isEditingName) {
    return (
      <CollectionRenameForm
        name={name}
        onChangeCollectionName={this.setCollectionName}
        onCancelCollectionNameChange=
        {this.toggleEditCollectionName}
      />
    );
  }

  return (
    <div>
```

```
    <Header text={this.getHeaderText()}/>

    <Button
      label="Rename collection"
      handleClick={this.toggleEditCollectionName}
    />

    <Button
      label="Empty collection"
      handleClick={onRemoveAllTweetsFromCollection}
    />

    <CollectionExportForm htmlMarkup={htmlMarkup}/>
  </div>
 );
}
```

First, we check whether the component state's `this.state.isEditingName`
property is set to `true`. If it is, then the `CollectionControls` component returns
the `CollectionRenameForm` component that renders a form to change the collection
name:

```
<CollectionRenameForm
  name={name}
  onChangeCollectionName={this.setCollectionName}
  onCancelCollectionNameChange={this.toggleEditCollectionName}
/>
```

The `CollectionRenameForm` component renders a form to change the collection
name. It receives three properties:

- The `name` property, which references the current collection name
- The `onChangeCollectionName` and `onCancelCollectionNameChange`
  properties, which reference the component's methods

We'll implement the `CollectionRenameForm` component later in this chapter. Now
let's take a closer look at the `setCollectionName` method:

```
setCollectionName = (name) => {
  this.setState({
    name,
    isEditingName: false
  });
}
```

The setCollectionName() method updates the collection's name and hides a form to edit the collection name by updating the component's state. We'll call this method when the user submits a new collection name.

Now, let's take a look at the toggleEditCollectionName() method:

```
toggleEditCollectionName = () => {
  this.setState(prevState => ({
    isEditingName: !prevState.isEditingName
  }));
}
```

This method shows or hides the collection's name editing form by setting the isEditingName property to the opposite of its current Boolean value using the ! operator. We'll call this method when the user clicks on the **Rename collection** or **Cancel** buttons, that is, show or hide the collection name change form.

If the CollectionControls component state's this.state.isEditingName property is set to false, then it returns collection controls:

```
return (
  <div>
    <Header text={this.getHeaderText()}/>

    <Button
      label="Rename collection"
      handleClick={this.toggleEditCollectionName}
    />

    <Button
      label="Empty collection"
      handleClick={onRemoveAllTweetsFromCollection}
    />

    <CollectionExportForm htmlMarkup={htmlMarkup}/>
  </div>
);
```

We wrap the Header component, two Button components, and the CollectionExportForm component in a div element. You're already familiar with the Header component from the previous chapter. It receives a text property that references a string. However, in this case, we do not directly pass a string, but rather a call to the this.getHeaderText() function:

```
<Header text={this.getHeaderText()} />
```

In turn, `this.getHeaderText()` returns a string. Let's take a closer look at the `getHeaderText()` method:

```
getHeaderText = () => {
  const { name } = this.state;
  const { numberOfTweetsInCollection } = this.props;
  let text = numberOfTweetsInCollection;

  if (numberOfTweetsInCollection === 1) {
    text = `${text} tweet in your`;
  } else {
    text = `${text} tweets in your`;
  }

  return (
    <span>
      {text} <strong>{name}</strong> collection
    </span>
  );
}
```

This method generates a string for our header based on the number of tweets in our collection. The important feature of this method is that it returns not only a string, but rather a tree of React elements that encapsulate that string. First, we create the `numberOfTweetsInCollection` constant. It stores the number of tweets in a collection. We then create a `text` variable and assign it a number of tweets in a collection. At this point, the `text` variable stores an integer value. Our next task is to concatenate the right string to it based on what that integer value is:

- If `numberOfTweetsInCollection` is 1, then we need to concatenate `' tweet in your'`

- Otherwise, we need to concatenate `' tweets in your'`

Once the header string is created, we then return the following elements:

```
return (
  <span>
    {text} <strong>{name}</strong> collection
  </span>
);
```

The final string encapsulated inside a `<span>` element consists of a value of a `text` variable, a collection name, and the `collection` keyword; consider this example:

```
1 tweet in your new collection.
```

Once this string is returned by the `getHeaderText()` method, it is then passed as a property to a `Header` component. Our next collection control element in the `CollectionControls` components `render()` method is `Button`:

```
<Button
  label="Rename collection"
  handleClick={this.toggleEditCollectionName}
/>
```

We pass the `Rename collection` string to its `label` property and the `this.toggleEditCollectionName` method to its `handleClick` property. As a result, this button will have the `Rename collection` label, and it will toggle a form to change the collection name.

The next collection control element is our second `Button` component:

```
<Button
  label="Empty collection"
  handleClick={onRemoveAllTweetsFromCollection}
/>
```

As you can guess, it will have an `Empty collection` label, and it will remove all the tweets from a collection.

Our final collection control element is `CollectionExportForm`:

```
<CollectionExportForm htmlMarkup={htmlMarkup} />
```

This element receives an HTML markup string that represents our collection, and it will render a button. We'll create this component later in this chapter.

Now, since you understand what the `CollectionControls` component will render, let's take a closer look at its child components. We'll start with the `CollectionRenameForm` component.

Creating the CollectionRenameForm component

First, let's create the ~/snapterest/source/components/CollectionRenameForm.js file:

```
import React, { Component } from 'react';
import Header from './Header';
import Button from './Button';

const inputStyle = {
  marginRight: '5px'
};

class CollectionRenameForm extends Component {
  constructor(props) {
    super(props);

    const { name } = props;

    this.state = {
      inputValue: name
    };
  }

  setInputValue = (inputValue) => {
    this.setState({
      inputValue
    });
  }

  handleInputValueChange = (event) => {
    const inputValue = event.target.value;
    this.setInputValue(inputValue);
  }

  handleFormSubmit = (event) => {
    event.preventDefault();

    const { onChangeCollectionName } = this.props;
    const { inputValue: collectionName } = this.state;
```

```
          onChangeCollectionName(collectionName);
    }

    handleFormCancel = (event) => {
      event.preventDefault();

      const {
        name: collectionName,
        onCancelCollectionNameChange
      } = this.props;

      this.setInputValue(collectionName);
      onCancelCollectionNameChange();
    }

    componentDidMount() {
      this.collectionNameInput.focus();
    }

    render() {
      const { inputValue } = this.state;

      return (
        <form className="form-inline" onSubmit={this.handleSubmit}>

          <Header text="Collection name:"/>
          <div className="form-group">
            <input
              className="form-control"
              style={inputStyle}
              onChange={this.handleInputValueChange}
              value={inputValue}
              ref={input => { this.collectionNameInput = input; }}
            />
          </div>

          <Button
            label="Change"
            handleClick={this.handleFormSubmit}
          />
          <Button
            label="Cancel"
            handleClick={this.handleFormCancel}
          />
```

```
      </form>
    );
  }
}

export default CollectionRenameForm;
```

This component renders a form to change the collection name:

```
render() {
  const { inputValue } = this.state;

  return (
    <form className="form-inline" onSubmit={this.handleSubmit}>

      <Header text="Collection name:"/>
      <div className="form-group">
        <input
          className="form-control"
          style={inputStyle}
          onChange={this.handleInputValueChange}
          value={inputValue}
          ref={input => this.collectionNameInput = input}
        />
      </div>

      <Button
        label="Change"
        handleClick={this.handleFormSubmit}
      />
      <Button
        label="Cancel"
        handleClick={this.handleFormCancel}
      />
    </form>
  );
}
```

Our `<form>` element wraps four elements, which are as follows:

- One `Header` component
- One `<input>` element
- Two `Button` components

The Header component renders the "Collection name:" string. The <input> element is wrapped inside a <div> element with a className property set to form-group. This name is part of the Bootstrap framework that we discussed in *Chapter 5, Making Your React Components Reactive*. It's used for layout and styling, and it's not part of our React application's logic.

The <input> element has quite a few properties. Let's take a closer look at it:

```
<input
  className="form-control"
  style={inputStyle}
  onChange={this.handleInputValueChange}
  value={inputValue}
  ref={input => { this.collectionNameInput = input; }}
/>
```

The following is the description of the properties used in the preceding code:

- The className property is set to form-control. It is another class name, which is part of the Bootstrap framework. We will use this for styling purposes.

- In addition, we apply our own style to this input element using the style property that references the inputStyle object with a single style rule, that is, marginRight.

- The value property is set to the current value stored in the component's state, this.state.inputValue.

- The onChange property references a handleInputValueChange method that is an onchange event handler.

- The ref property is a special React property that you can attach to any component. It takes a callback function, which React will execute immediately after the component is mounted and unmounted. It allows us to access the DOM input element that our React component renders.

I would like you to focus on the last three properties: value, onChange, and ref. The value property is set to the component state's property, and the only way to change that value is to update its state. On the other hand, we know that a user can interact with an input field and change its value. Will this behavior apply to our component? No. Whenever a user types, our input field's value won't change. This is because a component is in control of <input>, not the user. In our CollectionRenameForm component, the value of the <input> always reflects the value of the this.state.inputValue property, regardless of what the user types. The user is not in control, but the CollectionRenameForm component is.

Then, how can we make sure that our input field reacts to the user input? We need to listen to the user input, and update the state of the CollectionRenameForm component, which in turn will re-render the input field with an updated value. Doing so on every input's change event will make our input look like it works as usual, and the user can freely change its value.

For this, we provide our <input> element with the onChange property that references the component's this.handleInputValueChange method:

```
handleInputValueChange = (event) => {

    const inputValue = event.target.value;

    this.setInputValue(inputValue);

}
```

As we discussed in *Chapter 4, Creating Your First React Component*, React passes instances of SyntheticEvent to event handlers. The handleInputValueChange() method receives an event object with a target property that has a value property. This value property stores a string that a user has typed in our input field. We pass that string into our this.setInputValue() method:

```
setInputValue = (inputValue) => {
    this.setState({
        inputValue
    });
}
```

The setInputValue() method is a convenient method that updates the component's state with a new input value. In turn, this update will re-render the <input> element with an updated value.

What's the initial input's value when the CollectionRenameForm component is mounted? Let's take a look at this:

```
constructor(props) {
    super(props);

    const { name } = props;

    this.state = {
        inputValue: name
    };
}
```

As you can see, we pass the collection's name from a parent component, and we use it to set the component's initial state.

After we mount this component, we want to set focus on the input field so that the user can start editing the collection's name straightaway. We know that once a component is inserted into the DOM, React calls its `componentDidMount()` method. This method is our best opportunity to set `focus`:

```
componentDidMount() {
    this.collectionNameInput.focus();
}
```

To do this, we get our input element by referencing `this.collectionNameInput` and call the `focus()` function on it.

How can we reference a DOM element inside the `componentDidMount()` method? Remember that we provided the `ref` property to our `input` element. Then we passed a callback function to that `ref` property, which in turn assigned a reference to the DOM input element to `this.collectionNameInput`. So now we can get that reference by accessing the `this.collectionNameInput` property.

Finally, let's discuss our two form buttons:

- The `Change` button submits the form and changes the collection name
- The `Cancel` button submits the form, but doesn't change the collection name

We'll start with a `Change` button:

```
<Button
  label="Change"
  handleClick={this.handleFormSubmit}
/>
```

When a user clicks on it, the `this.handleFormSubmit` method is called:

```
handleFormSubmit = (event) => {
  event.preventDefault();

  const { onChangeCollectionName } = this.props;
  const { inputValue: collectionName } = this.state;

  onChangeCollectionName(collectionName);
}
```

We cancel the `submit` event, then get the collection name from the component's state, and pass it to the `this.props.onChangeCollectionName()` function call. The `onChangeCollectionName` function is passed by a parent `CollectionControls` component. Calling this function will change our collection's name.

Now let's discuss our second form button:

```
<Button
  label="Cancel"
  handleClick={this.handleFormCancel}
/>
```

When a user clicks on it, the `this.handleFormCancel` method is called:

```
handleFormCancel = (event) => {
  event.preventDefault();

  const {
    name: collectionName,
    onCancelCollectionNameChange
  } = this.props;

  this.setInputValue(collectionName);
  onCancelCollectionNameChange();
}
```

Once again, we cancel a `submit` event, then get the original collection name that is passed as a property by a parent `CollectionControls` component, and pass it to our `this.setInputValue()` function. Then, we call the `this.props.onCancelCollectionNameChange()` function that hides the collection controls.

That's our `CollectionRenameForm` component. Next, let's create our `Button` component that we reused twice in our `CollectionRenameForm` component.

Creating the Button component

Create the following `~/snapterest/source/components/Button.js` file:

```
import React from 'react';

const buttonStyle = {
  margin: '10px 0'
};

const Button = ({ label, handleClick }) => (
```

```
<button
  className="btn btn-default"
  style={buttonStyle}
  onClick={handleClick}
>
  {label}
</button>
);

export default Button;
```

The `Button` component renders a button.

Notice that we didn't declare a class, but rather defined a simple function called `Button`. This is the functional way of creating React components. In fact, when the purpose of your component is purely to render some user interface elements with or without any props, then it's recommended that you use this approach.

You can think of this simple React component as a "pure" function which takes an input in the form of the `props` object and returns JSX as output—consistently, no matter how many times you call this function.

Ideally, most of your components should be created that way—as "pure" JavaScript functions. Of course, this is not possible when your component has state, but for all stateless components—there's a chance! Now take a look at all the components that we've created so far and see if you can rewrite them as "pure" functions instead of using classes.

I recommend that you read more about functional versus class components at: `https://facebook.github.io/react/docs/components-and-props.html`

You might be wondering what's the benefit of creating a dedicated component for a button if you could just use the `<button>` element? Think of a component as a wrapper for a `<button>` element and something else that comes with it. In our case, most `<button>` elements come with the same style, so it makes sense to encapsulate both the `<button>` and style objects inside a component, and reuse that component. Hence, the dedicated `Button` component. It expects to receive two properties from a parent component:

- The `label` property is a label for a button
- The `handleClick` property is a callback function that is called when a user clicks on this button

Now, it's time to create our `CollectionExportForm` component.

Creating the CollectionExportForm component

The CollectionExportForm component is responsible for exporting a collection to a third-party website (http://codepen.io). Once your collection is on CodePen, you can save it and share it with your friends. Let's take a look at how this can be done.

Create the ~/snapterest/source/components/CollectionExportForm.js file:

```
import React from 'react';

const formStyle = {
  display: 'inline-block'
};

const CollectionExportForm = ({ htmlMarkup }) => (
  <form
      action="http://codepen.io/pen/define"
      method="POST"
      target="_blank"
      style={formStyle}
    >
      <input type="hidden" name="data" value={htmlMarkup}/>
      <button type="submit" className="btn btn-default">
        Export as HTML
      </button>
    </form>
);

export default CollectionExportForm;
```

The CollectionExportForm component renders a form with the <input> and <button> elements. The <input> element is hidden, and its value is set to an HTML markup string that is passed by a parent component as htmlMarkup property. The <button> element is the only element in this form that is visible to the user. When the user clicks on the **Export as HTML** button, a collection is submitted to CodePen that is opened in a new window. A user can then modify and share that collection.

Congratulations! At this point, you've built a fully functional web application with React. Let's see how it works.

First, make sure that Snapkite Engine that we installed and configured in *Chapter 2, Installing Powerful Tools for Your Project*, is running. Navigate to `~/snapkite-engine/` and run the following command:

```
npm start
```

Then, open a new Terminal window, navigate to `~/snapterest/`, and run this command:

```
npm start
```

Now open `~/snapterest/build/index.html` in your web browser. You will see new tweets appear. Click on them to add them to your collection. Click on them again to remove individual tweets from the collection. Click on the **Empty collection** button to remove all the tweets from your collection. Click on the **Rename collection** button, type a new collection name, and click on the **Change** button. Finally, click on the **Export as HTML** button to export your collection to `CodePen.io`. If you have any trouble with this chapter or previous chapters, then go to `https://github.com/fedosejev/react-essentials` and create a new issue.

Summary

In this chapter, you created the `TweetList`, `CollectionControls`, `CollectionRenameForm`, `CollectionExportForm`, and `Button` components. You completed building a fully functional React application.

In our next chapters, we'll test this application with Jest, and enhance it with Flux and Redux.

9
Testing Your React Application with Jest

By now, you have created a number of React components. Some of them are quite straightforward, but some are sophisticated enough. Having built both, you might have gained a certain confidence, which makes you believe that no matter how complex the user interface is, you can build it with React, without any major pitfalls. This is a good confidence to have. After all, this is why we're investing time in learning React. However, there is a trap that many confident React developers fall into—the act of not writing unit tests.

What is a **unit test**? As the name suggests, it's a test for a single unit of your application. A single unit in your application is often a function, which suggests that writing unit tests means writing tests for your functions.

Why write unit tests?

You might be wondering why you should write unit tests. Let me tell you a story from my personal experience. I released a website that I built recently. A few days later, my colleague who was using the website sent me an email with two files that the website kept rejecting. I closely examined the files, and the requirement of having the IDs matched was met in both of them. However, the files were still rejected and the error message said that the IDs didn't match. Can you guess what the problem was?

I wrote a function that checked whether the IDs from the two files matched. The function checked both the value and the type of the IDs, so if the values were the same and the types were different, it would return no match; it turned out that this was exactly the case with the files from my colleague.

The important question is, how can I prevent this from happening? The answer is a number of unit tests for my function.

Creating test suites, specs, and expectations

How does one write a test for JavaScript functions? You need a testing framework, and luckily, Facebook has built its own unit test framework for JavaScript, called **Jest**. It is inspired by **Jasmine** — another well-known JavaScript test framework. Those who are familiar with Jasmine will find Jest's approach to testing very similar. However, I'll make no assumptions about your prior experience with testing frameworks and discuss the basics first.

The fundamental idea of unit testing is that you test only one piece of functionality in your application that usually is implemented by one function. You test it in isolation, which means that all the other parts of your application that the function depends on are not used by your tests. Instead, they are imitated by your tests. To imitate a JavaScript object is to create a fake one that simulates the behavior of the real object. In unit testing, the fake object is called **mock** and the process of creating it is called **mocking**.

Jest automatically mocks the dependencies when you're running your tests. It automatically finds tests to be executed in your repository. Let's take a look at the following example.

First, create the `~/snapterest/source/utils/` directory. Then, create a new `TweetUtils.js` file in it:

```
function getListOfTweetIds(tweets) {
  return Object.keys(tweets);
}

export default { getListOfTweetIds };
```

The `TweetUtils.js` file is a module with the `getListOfTweetIds()` utility function for our application to use. Given an object with tweets, `getListOfTweetIds()` returns an array of tweet IDs.

Now let's write our first unit test with Jest. We'll test our `getListOfTweetIds()` function.

Create a `TweetUtils.test.js` file inside `~/snapterest/source/utils/`:

```
import TweetUtils from './TweetUtils';

describe('TweetUtils', () => {
  test('getListOfTweetIds returns an array of tweet ids', () => {
    const tweetsMock = {
```

```
      tweet1: {},
      tweet2: {},
      tweet3: {}
    };
    const expectedListOfTweetIds = [
      'tweet1',
      'tweet2',
      'tweet3'
    ];
    const actualListOfTweetIds = TweetUtils.getListOfTweetIds(
      tweetsMock
    );

    expect(actualListOfTweetIds)
      .toEqual(expectedListOfTweetIds);
  });
});
```

First, we require the `TweetUtils` module:

```
import TweetUtils from './TweetUtils';
```

Next, we call a global `describe()` Jest function. It's important to understand the concept behind it. In our `TweetUtils.test.js` file, we're not just creating a single test, instead we're creating a suite of tests. A suite is a collection of tests that collectively tests a bigger unit of functionality. For example, a suite can have multiple tests, which tests all the individual parts of a larger module. In our example, we have a `TweetUtils` module with potentially a number of utility functions. In this situation, we would create a suite for the `TweetUtils` module, and then create tests for each individual utility function, such as `getListOfTweetIds()`.

The `describe()` function defines a suite and takes these two parameters:

- **Suite name**: This is the title that describes what is being tested by this test suite

- **Suite implementation**: This is the function that implements this suite

In our example, the suite is as follows:

```
describe('TweetUtils', () => {
  // Test suite implementation goes here
});
```

How do you create an individual test? In Jest, you create individual tests by calling another global Jest function—`test()`. Just like `describe()`, the `test()` function takes two parameters:

- **Test name**: This is the title that describes what is being tested by this test, for example: `'getListOfTweetIds returns an array of tweet ids'`
- **Test implementation**: This is the function that implements this test

In our example, the test is as follows:

```
test('getListOfTweetIds returns an array of tweet ids', () => {
  // Test implementation goes here...
});
```

Let's take a closer look at the implementation of our test:

```
const tweetsMock = {
  tweet1: {},
  tweet2: {},
  tweet3: {}
};
const expectedListOfTweetIds = [
  'tweet1',
  'tweet2',
  'tweet3'
];
const actualListOfTweetIds = TweetUtils.getListOfTweetIds(
  tweetsMock
);

expect(actualListOfTweetIds)
  .toEqual(expectedListOfTweetIds);
```

We test whether the `getListOfTweetIds()` method of our `TweetUtils` module returns an array of tweet IDs, when given an object with tweet objects.

First, we will create a mock object that simulates the real tweets object:

```
const tweetsMock = {
  tweet1: {},
  tweet2: {},
  tweet3: {}
};
```

The only requirement for this mock object is to have tweet IDs as object keys. The values are not important, so we choose empty objects. The key names are not important as well, so we choose to name them tweet1, tweet2, and tweet3. This mock object doesn't fully simulate the real tweet object—its sole purpose is to simulate the fact that its keys are tweet IDs.

The next step is to create an expected list of tweet IDs:

```
const expectedListOfTweetIds = [
  'tweet1',
  'tweet2',
  'tweet3'
];
```

We know what tweet IDs to expect because we've mocked the tweets object with the same IDs.

The next step is to extract the actual tweet IDs from our mocked tweets object. For this, we use the getListOfTweetIds() method that takes the tweets object and returns an array of tweet IDs:

```
const actualListOfTweetIds = TweetUtils.getListOfTweetIds(
  tweetsMock
);
```

We pass the tweetsMock object to that method and store the results in the actualListOfTweetIds constant. The reason it's named actualListOfTweetIds is that this list of tweet IDs is produced by the actual getListOfTweetIds() function that we're testing.

The final step will introduce us to a new important concept:

```
expect(actualListOfTweetIds)
  .toEqual(expectedListOfTweetIds);
```

Let's think about the process of testing. We need to take an actual value produced by the method that we're testing, that is, getListOfTweetIds(), and match it to the expected value that we know in advance. The result of that match will determine whether our test has passed or failed.

The reason why we can guess what `getListOfTweetIds()` will return in advance is because we've prepared the input for it; this is our mock object:

```
const tweetsMock = {
  tweet1: {},
  tweet2: {},
  tweet3: {}
};
```

So, we can expect the following output by calling `TweetUtils.getListOfTweetIds(tweetsMock)`:

```
[ 'tweet1', 'tweet2', 'tweet3' ]
```

Because something can go wrong inside `getListOfTweetIds()`, we cannot guarantee this result; we can only *expect* it.

This is why we need to create an expectation. In Jest, an **expectation** is built using the `expect()` function, which takes an actual value; for example, the `actualListOfTweetIds` object: `expect(actualListOfTweetIds)`.

Then, we chain it with a **matcher** function that compares the actual value with the expected value and tells Jest whether the expectation was met or not:

```
expect(actualListOfTweetIds)
  .toEqual(expectedListOfTweetIds);
```

In our example, we use the `toEqual()` matcher function to compare the two arrays. You can find a list of all the built-in matcher functions in Jest at `https://facebook.github.io/jest/docs/expect.html`

This is how you write a test. A test contains one or more expectations. Each expectation tests the state of your code. A test can be either a **passing test** or a **failing test**. A test is a passing test only when all the expectations are met; otherwise, it's a failing test.

Well done, you've written your first test suite with a single test that has one expectation! How can you run it?

Installing and running Jest

First, let's install the **Jest command-line interface (Jest CLI)** module:

```
npm install --save-dev jest
```

This command installs and adds the Jest module as a development dependency to our `~/snapterest/package.json` file.

In *Chapter 2*, *Installing Powerful Tools for Your Project*, we installed and discussed Babel. We use Babel to transpile our newer JavaScript syntax into the older JavaScript syntax, as well as compile JSX syntax into plain JavaScript syntax. In our tests, we'll be testing React components written in JSX syntax, but Jest doesn't understand JSX syntax out of the box. We need to tell Jest to automatically compile our tests with Babel. To do this, we need to install the `babel-jest` module:

```
npm install --save-dev babel-jest
```

Now we need to configure Babel. To do this, create the following `.babelrc` file in the `~/snapterest/` directory:

```
{
    "presets": ["es2015", "react"]
```

Next, let's edit the `package.json` file. We'll replace the existing `"scripts"` object:

```
"scripts": {
    "test": "echo \"Error: no test specified\" && exit 1"
},
```

Replace the preceding object with the following one:

```
"scripts": {
    "test": "jest"
},
```

Now we're ready to run our test suite. Navigate to the `~/snapterest/` directory, and run the following command:

```
npm test
```

You should see the following message in your Terminal window:

```
PASS   source/utils/TweetUtils.test.js
```

This output message tells you the following:

- `PASS`: Your test has passed
- `source/utils/TweetUtils.test.js`: Jest ran tests from this file

That's all it takes to write and test a tiny unit test. Now, let's create another one!

Creating multiple tests and expectations

This time, we'll create and test the collection utility module. Create the
`CollectionUtils.js` file in the `~/snapterest/source/utils/` directory:

```
import TweetUtils from './TweetUtils';

function getNumberOfTweetsInCollection(collection) {
  const listOfCollectionTweetIds = TweetUtils
    .getListOfTweetIds(collection);

  return listOfCollectionTweetIds.length;
}

function isEmptyCollection(collection) {
  return getNumberOfTweetsInCollection(collection) === 0;
}

export default {
  getNumberOfTweetsInCollection,
  isEmptyCollection
};
```

The `CollectionUtils` module has two functions:
`getNumberOfTweetsInCollection()` and `isEmptyCollection()`.

First, let's discuss `getNumberOfTweetsInCollection()`:

```
function getNumberOfTweetsInCollection(collection) {
  const listOfCollectionTweetIds = TweetUtils
    .getListOfTweetIds(collection);

  return listOfCollectionTweetIds.length;
}
```

As you can see, this function calls the `getListOfTweetIds()` method from the
`TweetUtils` module and passes the `collection` object as a parameter. The result
returned by `getListOfTweetIds()` is stored in the `listOfCollectionTweetIds`
constant, and since it's an array, `getNumberOfTweetsInCollection()` returns a
`length` property of that array.

Now, let's take a look at the `isEmptyCollection()` method:

```
function isEmptyCollection(collection) {
  return getNumberOfTweetsInCollection(collection) === 0;
}
```

This method reuses the `getNumberOfTweetsInCollection()` method
that we just discussed. It checks whether the result returned by a call to
`getNumberOfTweetsInCollection()` is equal to zero. Then, it returns the result of
that check, which is either `true` or `false`.

Notice that we export both methods from this module:

```
export default {
  getNumberOfTweetsInCollection,
  isEmptyCollection
};
```

We just created our `CollectionUtils` module. Our next task is to test it.

Inside the `~/snapterest/source/utils/` directory, create the following
`CollectionUtils.test.js` file:

```
import CollectionUtils from './CollectionUtils';

describe('CollectionUtils', () => {
  const collectionTweetsMock = {
    collectionTweet7: {},
    collectionTweet8: {},
    collectionTweet9: {}
  };

  test('getNumberOfTweetsInCollection returns a number of tweets
  in collection', () => {
    const actualNumberOfTweetsInCollection = CollectionUtils
    .getNumberOfTweetsInCollection(collectionTweetsMock);
    const expectedNumberOfTweetsInCollection = 3;

    expect(actualNumberOfTweetsInCollection)
    .toBe(expectedNumberOfTweetsInCollection);
  });

  test('isEmptyCollection checks if collection is not empty',
  () => {
    const actualIsEmptyCollectionValue = CollectionUtils
      .isEmptyCollection(collectionTweetsMock);

    expect(actualIsEmptyCollectionValue).toBeDefined();
    expect(actualIsEmptyCollectionValue).toBe(false);
    expect(actualIsEmptyCollectionValue).not.toBe(true);
  });
});
```

First we define our test suite:

```
describe('CollectionUtils', () => {
  const collectionTweetsMock = {
    collectionTweet7: {},
    collectionTweet8: {},
    collectionTweet9: {}
  };

  // Tests go here...
});
```

We give our test suite the name of the module that we're testing—`CollectionUtils`. Now let's take a look at the implementation of this test suite. Instead of immediately defining test specs like we did in our previous test suite, we're creating the `collectionTweetsMock` object. So, are we allowed to do this? Absolutely. The test suite implementation function is just another JavaScript function, where we can do some work before we define our test specs.

This test suite will implement more than one test. All of our tests will use the `collectionTweetsMock` object, so it makes sense to define it outside the specs' scope and reuse it inside the specs. As you might have already guessed, the `collectionTweetsMock` object imitates a collection of tweets.

Now let's implement the individual test specs.

Our first spec tests whether the `CollectionUtils` module returns a number of tweets in the collection:

```
test('getNumberOfTweetsInCollection returns a number
 of tweets in collection', () => {
  const actualNumberOfTweetsInCollection = CollectionUtils
    .getNumberOfTweetsInCollection(collectionTweetsMock);
  const expectedNumberOfTweetsInCollection = 3;

  expect(actualNumberOfTweetsInCollection)
    .toBe(expectedNumberOfTweetsInCollection);
});
```

We first get the actual number of tweets in our mock collection:

```
const actualNumberOfTweetsInCollection = CollectionUtils
    .getNumberOfTweetsInCollection(collectionTweetsMock);
```

For this, we call the `getNumberOfTweetsInCollection()` method and pass the `collectionTweetsMock` object to it. Then, we define the number of expected tweets in our mock collection:

```
const expectedNumberOfTweetsInCollection = 3;
```

Finally, we call the `expect()` global function to create an expectation:

```
expect(actualNumberOfTweetsInCollection)
    .toBe(expectedNumberOfTweetsInCollection);
```

We use the `toBe()` matcher function to match the actual value and the expected one.

If you now run the `npm test` command, you will see that both the test suites pass:

PASS   source/utils/CollectionUtils.test.js

PASS   source/utils/TweetUtils.test.js

Remember that for a test suite to pass, it must have only the passing specs. For a spec to pass, it must have all its expectations to be met. This is the case so far.

How about running a little evil experiment?

Open your `~/snapterest/source/utils/CollectionUtils.js` file, and inside the `getNumberOfTweetsInCollection()` function, go to the following line of code:

```
return listOfCollectionTweetIds.length;
```

Now change it to this:

```
return listOfCollectionTweetIds.length + 1;
```

What this tiny update will do is return an incorrect number of tweets in any given collection. Now run `npm test` once more. You should see that all your specs in `CollectionUtils.test.js` have failed. Here is the one we're interested in:

```
FAIL   source/utils/CollectionUtils.test.js

  CollectionUtils > getNumberOfTweetsInCollection returns
  a number of tweets in collection

    expect(received).toBe(expected)

    Expected value to be (using ===):
      3
    Received:
      4


    at Object.<anonymous> (source/utils/CollectionUtils.test.js:14:46)
```

We haven't seen a failing test before, so let's take a closer look at what it's trying to tell us.

First, it gives us the bad news that the `CollectionUtils.test.js` test has failed:

```
FAIL   source/utils/CollectionUtils.test.js
```

Then, it tells us in a human-friendly manner which test has failed:

```
  CollectionUtils > getNumberOfTweetsInCollection returns a number of
  tweets in collection
```

Then, what went wrong—the unexpected test result:

```
expect(received).toBe(expected)
    Expected value to be (using ===):
      3
    Received:
      4
```

Finally, Jest prints a stack trace that should give us enough technical details to quickly identify which part of our code has produced the unexpected result:

```
at Object.<anonymous> (source/utils/CollectionUtils.test.js:14:46)
```

Alright! Enough of failing our tests on purpose. Let's revert our `~/snapterest/source/utils/CollectionUtils.js` file to this:

```
return listOfCollectionTweetIds.length;
```

A test suite in Jest can have many specs that test different methods from a single module. Our `CollectionUtils` module has two methods. Now let's discuss the second one.

Our next spec in `CollectionUtils.test.js` checks whether the collection is not empty:

```
test('isEmptyCollection checks if collection is not empty', () => {
    const actualIsEmptyCollectionValue = CollectionUtils
      .isEmptyCollection(collectionTweetsMock);

    expect(actualIsEmptyCollectionValue).toBeDefined();
    expect(actualIsEmptyCollectionValue).toBe(false);
    expect(actualIsEmptyCollectionValue).not.toBe(true);
});
```

First, we call the `isEmptyCollection()` method and pass the `collectionTweetsMock` object to it. We store the result in the `actualIsEmptyCollectionValue` constant. Notice how we're reusing the same `collectionTweetsMock` object, as in our previous spec.

Next, we create not one but three expectations:

```
expect(actualIsEmptyCollectionValue).toBeDefined();
expect(actualIsEmptyCollectionValue).toBe(false);
expect(actualIsEmptyCollectionValue).not.toBe(true);
```

You might have already guessed what we're expecting from our `actualIsEmptyCollectionValue` constant.

First of all, we expect our collection to be defined:

```
expect(actualIsEmptyCollectionValue).toBeDefined();
```

This means that the `isEmptyCollection()` function must return something other than `undefined`.

Next, we expect its value to be `false`:

```
expect(actualIsEmptyCollectionValue).toBe(false);
```

Earlier, we used the `toEqual()` matcher function to compare the arrays. The `toEqual()` method does a deep comparison, which is perfect for comparing arrays, but it is an overkill for primitive values such as `false`.

Finally, we expect `actualIsEmptyCollectionValue` not to be `true`:

```
expect(actualIsEmptyCollectionValue).not.toBe(true);
```

The next comparison is inversed by `.not`. It matches the expectation with the inverse of `toBe(true)` with `false`.

Notice that `toBe(false)` and `not.toBe(true)` produce the same result.

Only when all the three expectations are met, does this spec pass.

So far, we've tested the utility modules, but how do you test the React components with Jest?

We'll find out next.

Testing React components

Let's step back from writing code for a minute and talk about what it means to test the user interface. What exactly are we testing? We're testing the fact that our user interface renders as expected. In other words, if we tell React to render a button, we expect it to render a button—not more, not less.

Now how can we check that this is the case? One way of doing this is to write a React component, bundle our application, run it in a web browser, and see with our own eyes that it displays what we want it to display. This is manual testing and we do it at least once. But it is time consuming and unreliable in the long term.

How can we automate this process? Jest can do most of the work for us, but Jest doesn't have it's own eyes, so it will need to borrow our eyes at least once for each component. If Jest "can't see" the result of rendering a React component, then how can it even test a React component?

In *Chapter 3, Creating Your First React Element*, we discussed React elements. They are plain JavaScript objects that describe what we want to see on the screen.

For example, consider this HTML markup:

```
<h1>Testing</h1>
```

This can be represented by the following plain JavaScript object:

```
{
  type: 'h1',
  children: 'Testing'
}
```

Having plain and simple JavaScript objects that represent the output that our components produce when we render them allows us to describe certain expectations about our components and their behavior. Let's see this in action.

The first React component that we'll test will be our `Header` component. Create the `Header.test.js` file in the `~/snapterest/source/components/` directory:

```
import React from 'react';
import renderer from 'react-test-renderer';
import Header, { DEFAULT_HEADER_TEXT } from './Header';

describe('Header', () => {
  test('renders default header text', () => {
    const component = renderer.create(
      <Header/>
    );

    const tree = component.toJSON();
    const firstChild = tree.children[0];

    expect(firstChild).toBe(DEFAULT_HEADER_TEXT);
  });

  test('renders provided header text', () => {
    const headerText = 'Testing';

    const component = renderer.create(
      <Header text={headerText} />
    );

    const tree = component.toJSON();
    const firstChild = tree.children[0];

    expect(firstChild).toBe(headerText);
  });
});
```

By now, you can recognize the structure of our test files. First, we define our test suite, and we give it the name `Header`. Our test suite has two test specs named `renders default header text` and `renders provided header text`. As their names suggest, they test that our `Header` component can render both the default and provided text. Let's take a closer look at this test suite.

First, we import the React module:

```
import React from 'react';
```

Then, we import the `react-test-renderer` module:

```
import renderer from 'react-test-renderer';
```

A React renderer renders React components to pure JavaScript objects. It doesn't require the DOM, so we can use it to render React components outside of a web browser. It works great with Jest. Let's install it:

npm install --save-dev react-test-renderer

Next, in order to test our `Header` component, we need to import it:

```
import Header, { DEFAULT_HEADER_TEXT } from './Header';
```

We're also importing `DEFAULT_HEADER_TEXT` from our `Header` module. We do this because we don't want to hardcode the actual string value that is the default header text. It would add extra work for maintaining this value. Instead, since out `Header` component knows what this value is, we're going to import and reuse it in our test.

Let's take a look at our first test named `renders default header text`. Our first task in this test is to render the `Header` component to the plain JavaScript object. The `react-test-renderer` module has the `create` method that does exactly this:

```
const component = renderer.create(
  <Header/>
);
```

We pass the `<Header/>` element to the `create()` function as an argument and we get back a JavaScript object that represents an instance of our `Header` component. It's not a simple representation of our component yet, so our next step is to convert that object into a simple tree representation of our component using the `toJSON` method:

```
const tree = component.toJSON();
```

Now, `tree` is a JavaScript object as well, but it's also a simple representation of our `Header` component that we can easily read and understand:

```
{ type: 'h2', props: {}, children: [ 'Default header' ] }
```

I recommend that you log both the `component` and `tree` objects and see how different they are:

```
console.log(component);
console.log(tree);
```

You'll quickly see that the `component` object is for React's internal use—it's hard to read and tell what it represents. On the other hand, the `tree` object is very easy to read and it's clear what it represents.

As you can see, our approach for testing React components so far is to convert `<Header/>` to `{ type: 'h2', props: {}, children: [ 'Default header' ] }`. Now that we have a simple JavaScript object that represents our component, we can check that this object has the expected values. If it does, we can conclude that our component will render in a web browser as expected. If it doesn't, then we might have introduced a bug.

When we render our `Header` component without any properties, `<Header/>`, we expect it to render a default text: `'Default header'`. To check that this is indeed the case, we need to access the `children` property from a tree representation of our `Header` component:

```
const firstChild = tree.children[0];
```

We expect our `Header` component to only have one child, so the text element will be the first child.

Now it's time to write our expectation:

```
expect(firstChild).toBe(DEFAULT_HEADER_TEXT);
```

Here we expect `firstChild` to have the same value as `DEFAULT_HEADER_TEXT`. Behind the scenes, `toBe` matcher uses `===` to do the comparison.

This is it for our first test!

In our second test named `'renders provided header text'`, we're testing that our `Header` component has the custom test that we provide via the `text` property:

```
test('renders provided header text', () => {
  const headerText = 'Testing';

  const component = renderer.create(
    <Header text={headerText}/>
  );

  const tree = component.toJSON();
```

```
    const firstChild = tree.children[0];

    expect(firstChild).toBe(headerText);
  });
```

Now you understand the core idea behind testing React components:

1. Render your component to the JavaScript object representation.
2. Find some value on that object and check that this value is what you expect.

As you can see, this is quite straightforward when your components are simple. But what if you need to test components that are composed of other components and so on? Imagine how complex the JavaScript object that represents that component will be. It will have many properties that are deeply nested. You might end up writing and maintaining a lot of code for accessing and comparing deeply nested values. This is when writing unit tests becomes too expensive and some developers might choose to give up on testing their components altogether.

Luckily there're two solutions available for us.

Here's one of them. Remember, when traversing and mutating DOM directly was too much work, so jQuery library was created to simplify that process? Well, for React components we have **Enzyme**—a JavaScript testing utility library from AirBnB that simplifies the process of traversing and manipulating the output produced from rendering React components.

Enzyme is a separate library from Jest. Let's install it:

```
npm install --save-dev enzyme jest-enzyme react-addons-test-utils
```

To use Enzyme together with Jest, we need to install three modules. Remember that Jest runs our tests, whereas Enzyme will help us to write our expectations.

Now let's rewrite our tests for our `Header` component using Enzyme:

```
    import React from 'react';
    import { shallow } from 'enzyme';
    import Header, { DEFAULT_HEADER_TEXT } from './Header';

    describe('Header', () => {
      test('renders default header text', () => {
        const wrapper = shallow(
          <Header/>
        );

        expect(wrapper.find('h2')).toHaveLength(1);
```

```
      expect(wrapper.contains(DEFAULT_HEADER_TEXT)).toBe(true);
    });

    test('renders provided header text', () => {
      const headerText = 'Testing';

      const wrapper = shallow(
        <Header text={headerText} />
      );

      expect(wrapper.find('h2')).toHaveLength(1);
      expect(wrapper.contains(headerText)).toBe(true);
    });
  });
```

First, we import the `shallow` function from the `enzyme` module:

```
import { shallow } from 'enzyme';
```

Then, inside of our test, we call the `shallow` function and pass our `Header`
component as an argument:

```
const wrapper = shallow(
  <Header/>
);
```

What we get in return is an object that wraps the result of rendering our `Header`
component. This object is created by Enzyme's `ShallowWrapper` class and has some
very useful methods for us to use. We'll call it `wrapper`.

Now that we have this `wrapper` object available to us, we're ready to write our
expectations. Notice that unlike `react-test-renderer`, with Enzyme we don't need
to convert our `wrapper` object into a simplified representation of our component.
This is because we're not going to traverse our `wrapper` object directly — it's not a
simple object that is easy for us to read; try to log that object and see it for yourself.
Instead, we'll use methods provided by Enzyme's `ShallowWrapper` API.

Let's write our first expectation:

```
expect(wrapper.find('h2')).toHaveLength(1);
```

As you can see, we're calling the `find` method on our `wrapper` object. This is the power of Enzyme. Instead of traversing our React component output object directly and finding the nested elements, we can simply call the `find` method and tell it what we're looking for. In this example, we're telling Enzyme to find all `h2` elements inside of our `wrapper` object, and since it wraps the output of our `Header` component, we expect the `wrapper` object to have exactly one `h2` element. We use Jest's `toHaveLength` matcher to check this.

Here's our second expectation:

```
expect(wrapper.contains(DEFAULT_HEADER_TEXT)).toBe(true);
```

As you can guess, we're checking that our wrapper object contains `DEFAULT_HEADER_TEXT`. This check allows us to conclude that our `Header` component renders the default text when we don't provide any custom text. We're using Enzyme's `contains` method that allows us to conveniently check if our component contains any node. In this case, we're checking for a text node.

Enzyme's API provides many more methods for us to conveniently inspect our component's output. I recommend that you familiarize yourself with those methods by reading the official documentation: `http://airbnb.io/enzyme/docs/api/shallow.html`

You might be wondering how to test the behavior of your React component.

This is what we'll discuss next!

Create the `Button.test.js` file in the `~/snapterest/source/components/` directory:

```
import React from 'react';
import { shallow } from 'enzyme';
import Button from './Button';

describe('Button', () => {
  test('calls click handler function on click', () => {
    const handleClickMock = jest.fn();

    const wrapper = shallow(
      <Button handleClick={handleClickMock}/>
    );

    wrapper.find('button').simulate('click');

    expect(handleClickMock.mock.calls.length).toBe(1);
  });
});
```

The `Button.test.js` file will test our `Button` component, and specifically, check whether it triggers the click event handler function when you click on it. Without further ado, let's focus on the `'calls click handler function on click'` spec implementation:

```
const handleClickMock = jest.fn();

const wrapper = shallow(
  <Button handleClick={handleClickMock} />
);

wrapper.find('button').simulate('click');

expect(handleClickMock.mock.calls.length).toBe(1);
```

In this spec, we're testing that our `Button` component calls a function that we provide via the `handleClick` property. Here's our testing strategy:

1. Generate a mock function.
2. Render the `Button` component with our mock function.
3. Find the `button` element in a wrapper object created by Enzyme as a result of rendering our `Button` component.
4. Simulate a click event on that `button` element.
5. Check whether our mock function was called exactly once.

Now that we have a plan, let's implement it. Let's create a mock function first:

```
const handleClickMock = jest.fn();
```

The `jest.fn()` function call returns the newly generated Jest mock function; we name it `handleClickMock`.

Next, we get the output of our `Button` component by calling Enzyme's `shallow` function:

```
const wrapper = shallow(
  <Button handleClick={handleClickMock}/>
);
```

We pass our `handleClickMock` function as a property to our `Button` component.

Then, we find the `button` element and we simulate a click event on it:

```
wrapper.find('button').simulate('click');
```

At this point, our button element is expected to call its `onClick` event handler, which, in this case is our `handleClickMock` function. This mock function should record the fact that it was called one time, or at least this is how we expect our `Button` component to behave. Let's create this expectation:

```
expect(handleClickMock.mock.calls.length).toBe(1);
```

How do we check how many times our `handleClickMock` function was called? Our `handleClickMock` function has a special mock property that we can inspect to find out how many times `handleClickMock` was called:

```
handleClickMock.mock.calls.length
```

In turn, our `mock` object has a `calls` object that knows everything about every call made to our `handleClickMock` function. The `calls` object is an array and in our case we expect its `length` property to equal to 1.

As you can see, with Enzyme it's easier to write expectations. Our tests require less work to write them in the first place and maintain them for the long term. This is good because now we have more motivation to write more tests.

But can we make writing tests with Jest even easier?

Turns out that we can.

Right now we render a React component into an object representation, and then inspect that object either with Jest only or with the help of Enzyme. This inspection requires us, as developers, to write extra code for our tests to work. How can we avoid that?

We can render a React component into a text string that we could easily read and understand. Then we can store that text representation in our code base. Later, when we run our tests again, we can simply create a new text representation and compare it with the one that we're storing. If they're different, then this could mean that either we updated our component intentionally and now we need to update our text representation as well, or we introduced a bug to our component so that now it produces an unexpected text representation.

This idea is called **snapshot testing** in Jest. Let's rewrite tests for our `Header` component using snapshot testing. Replace the existing code in your `Header.test.js` file with this new code:

```
import React from 'react';
import renderer from 'react-test-renderer';
import Header from './Header';

describe('Header', () => {
```

```
test('renders default header text', () => {
  const component = renderer.create(
    <Header/>
  );

  const tree = component.toJSON();

  expect(tree).toMatchSnapshot();
});

test('renders provided header text', () => {
  const headerText = 'Testing';

  const component = renderer.create(
    <Header text={headerText} />
  );

  const tree = component.toJSON();

  expect(tree).toMatchSnapshot();
});
});
```

As you can see, we're not using Enzyme in this case, which should make sense to us, because we don't want to inspect anything anymore.

On the other hand, we're using the `react-test-renderer` module again to render and convert our components into a simple JavaScript object that we named `tree`:

```
const component = renderer.create(
  <Header/>
);

const tree = component.toJSON();
```

The key line of code that puts snapshot testing in action is this line:

```
expect(tree).toMatchSnapshot();
```

We're simply telling Jest that we expect our tree object to match to an existing snapshot. Wait a minute, but we don't have an existing snapshot. Good observation! So what happens in this case? Jest won't find an existing snapshot for this test, and instead it will create a very first snapshot for this test.

Let's run our test command:

npm test

All tests should pass and you should see this output:

Snapshot Summary

> **2 snapshots written in 1 test suite.**

Here Jest is telling us that it created two snapshots—one for each test found in our `Header.test.js` test suite. Where did Jest store these two snapshots? If you check your `~/snapterest/source/components/` directory, you will find a new folder there: `__snapshots__`. Inside it, you'll find the `Header.test.js.snap` file. Open this file and look at its contents:

```
// Jest Snapshot v1, https://goo.gl/fbAQLP

exports[`Header renders default header text 1`] = `
<h2
  style={
    Object {
      "display": "inline-block",
      "fontSize": "16px",
      "fontWeight": "300",
      "margin": "20px 10px",
    }
  }
>
  Default header
</h2>
`;

exports[`Header renders provided header text 1`] = `
<h2
  style={
    Object {
      "display": "inline-block",
      "fontSize": "16px",
      "fontWeight": "300",
      "margin": "20px 10px",
    }
  }
>
  Testing
</h2>
`;
```

What you can see in this file is the text representation of the output that our `Header` component produces when we render it with Jest. It's very easy for us to read this file and confirm that this is what we expect our `Header` component to render. Now our `Header` component has its own snapshots. It's important to treat and store these snapshots as part of your source code.

You should commit them to your Git repository if you have one and you should be aware of any changes that you're making to them.

Now that you've seen three different ways of writing React tests, you need to make your own choice of how to test your React components. Now I would recommend that you use snapshot testing and Enzyme.

Great, we've written four test suites. Now it's time to run all our tests.

Navigate to `~/snapterest/` and run this command:

`npm test`

All your test suites should PASS:

```
PASS   source/components/Button.test.js

PASS   source/components/Header.test.js

PASS   source/utils/CollectionUtils.test.js

PASS   source/utils/TweetUtils.test.js


Snapshot Summary
  › 2 snapshots written in 1 test suite.


Test Suites: 4 passed, 4 total
Tests:       6 passed, 6 total
Snapshots:   2 added, 2 total
Time:        2.461s
Ran all test suites.
```

Log messages, such as these, will help you sleep well at night and go on holidays, without the need to constantly check your work emails.

Well done!

Summary

Now you know how to create the React components and unit test them.

In this chapter, you learned the essentials of Jest—the unit testing framework from Facebook that works well with React. You got introduced to the Enzyme library and learned how it simplifies writing unit tests for React components. We discussed the test suites, specs, expectations, and matchers. We created mocks and simulated click events.

In the next chapter, you'll learn the essentials of the Flux architecture and how to improve the maintainability of our React application.

10
Supercharging Your React Architecture with Flux

The process of building a web application has one quality that somewhat mirrors the process of evolution of life itself—it never ends. Unlike building a bridge, building a web application has no natural state that represents the end of the development process. It's up to you or your team to decide when you should stop the development process and release what you've already built.

In this book, we've reached the point at which we can stop developing Snapterest. Right now, we have a small React.js application with a basic functionality that simply works.

Isn't that enough?

Not exactly. Earlier in this book, we discussed how the process of maintaining your web application is much more expensive in terms of time and effort than the process of developing it. If we choose to finish developing Snapterest at its current state, we'll also choose to start the process of maintaining it.

Are we ready to maintain Snapterest? Do we know if its current state will allow us to introduce new functionality later on without any significant code refactoring?

Analyzing your web application's architecture

To answer these questions, let's zoom out from the implementation details and explore our application's architecture:

- The app.js file renders our Application component
- The Application component manages a collection of tweets and renders our Stream and Collection components
- The Stream component receives the new tweets from the SnapkiteStreamClient library and renders the StreamTweet and Header components
- The Collection component renders the CollectionControls and TweetList components

Stop right there. Can you tell how data flows inside our application? Do you know where it enters our application? How does a new tweet end up in our collection? Let's examine our data flow more closely:

1. We use the SnapkiteStreamClient library to receive a new tweet inside a Stream component.
2. This new tweet is then passed from Stream to the StreamTweet component.
3. The StreamTweet component passes it to the Tweet component, which renders the tweet image.
4. A user clicks on that tweet image to add it to its collection.
5. The Tweet component passes the tweet object to the StreamTweet component via the handleImageClick(tweet) callback function.
6. The StreamTweet component passes that tweet object to the Stream component via the onAddTweetToCollection(tweet) callback function.
7. The Stream component passes that tweet object to the Application component via the onAddTweetToCollection(tweet) callback function.
8. The Application component adds tweet to the collectionTweets object and updates its state.
9. The state update triggers the Application component to re-render, which in turn re-renders the Collection component with an updated collection of tweets.
10. Then, the child components of the Collection component can mutate our collection of tweets as well.

Do you feel confused? Can you rely on this architecture in the long run? Do you think it's easily maintainable? I don't think so.

Let's identify the key problems with our current architecture. We can see that the new data enters our React application via the Stream component. It then travels all the way down to the Tweet component in the component hierarchy. Then, it travels all the way up to the Application component, where it's stored and managed.

Why do we store and manage our collection tweets in the Application component? Because Application is a parent component for two other components: Stream and Collection. Both of them need to be able to mutate our collection tweets. In order to accommodate this, our Application component needs to pass callback functions to both the components:

- The Stream component:

```
<Stream
  onAddTweetToCollection={this.addTweetToCollection}
/>
```

- The Collection component:

```
<Collection
  tweets={collectionTweets}
  onRemoveTweetFromCollection=
  {this.removeTweetFromCollection}
  onRemoveAllTweetsFromCollection=
  {this.removeAllTweetsFromCollection}
/>
```

The Stream component gets the onAddTweetToCollection() function to add a tweet to the collection. The Collection component gets the onRemoveTweetFromCollection() function to remove a tweet from the collection, and the onRemoveAllTweetsFromCollection() function to remove all the tweets from the collection.

These callback functions are then propagated down to the component hierarchy until they reach some component that actually calls them. In our application, the onAddTweetToCollection() function is only called in the Tweet component. Let's take a look at how many times it needs to be passed from one component to another before it can be called in a Tweet component:

```
Application > Stream > StreamTweet > Tweet
```

The onAddTweetToCollection() function is not used in the Stream and StreamTweet components, yet both of them get it as a property for the purpose of passing it down to their child components.

Snapterest is a small React application, so this problem is rather an inconvenience, but later on, if you decide to add new features, this inconvenience will quickly become a maintenance nightmare:

```
Application > ComponentA > ComponentB > ComponentC > ComponentD >
ComponentE > ComponentF > ComponentG > Tweet
```

To prevent this from happening, we're going to solve two problems:

- We'll change how the new data enters our application
- We'll change how the components get and set data

We'll rethink of how data flows inside our application with the help of Flux.

Understanding Flux

Flux is the application architecture from Facebook that complements React. It's not a framework or a library, but rather a solution to a common problem — how to build scalable client-side applications.

With the Flux architecture, we can rethink how data flows inside of our application. Flux makes sure that all our data flows only in a **single direction**. This helps us to reason about how our application works, regardless of how small or large it is. With Flux, we can add new functionality without exploding our application's complexity or its mental model.

You might have noticed that both React and Flux share the same core concept — one-way data flow. This is why they naturally work well together. We know how data flows inside of a React component, but how does Flux implement the one-way data flow?

With Flux, we separate the concerns of our application into four logical entities:

- Actions
- Dispatchers
- Stores
- Views

Actions are objects that we create when we want to change our application's state. For example, when our application receives a new tweet, we create a new action. An action object has a `type` property that identifies what action it is and any other properties that our application needs to transition to a new state. Here is an example of an action object:

```
const action = {
  type: 'receive_tweet',
  tweet
};
```

As you can see, this is an action of the `receive_tweet` type, and it has the `tweet` property, which is a new tweet object that our application has received. You can guess what change in your application's state this action represents by looking at the action's type. For each new tweet that our application receives, it creates a `receive_tweet` action.

Where does this action go? What part of our application gets this action? Actions are dispatched to stores.

Stores are responsible for managing your application's data. They provide methods for accessing that data, but not for changing it. If you want to change data in stores, you have to create and dispatch an action.

We know how to create an action, but how do you dispatch it? As the name suggests, you can use a dispatcher for this.

The dispatcher is responsible for dispatching all the actions to all stores:

- All store register with a dispatcher. They provide a callback function.
- All actions are dispatched by a dispatcher to all stores that did register with a dispatcher.

This is how data flow looks like in the Flux architecture:

```
Actions > Dispatcher > Stores
```

You can see that the dispatcher plays a role of a central element in our data flow. All actions are dispatched by it. Stores register with it. All the actions are dispatched synchronously. You can't dispatch an action in the middle of the previous action dispatch. No action can skip the dispatcher in the Flux architecture.

Creating a dispatcher

Now let's implement this data flow. We'll start by creating a dispatcher first. Facebook offers us its implementation of a dispatcher that we can reuse. Let's take advantage of this:

1. Navigate to the `~/snapterest` directory and run the following command:

   ```
   npm install --save flux
   ```

   The `flux` module comes with a `Dispatcher` function that we'll be reusing.

2. Next, create a new folder called `dispatcher` in our project's `~/snapterest/source/dispatcher` directory. Now create the `AppDispatcher.js` file in it:

   ```
   import { Dispatcher } from 'flux';
   export default new Dispatcher();
   ```

First, we import `Dispatcher` provided by Facebook, then create, and export a new instance of it. Now we can use this instance in our application.

Next, we need a convenient way of creating and dispatching actions. For each action, let's create a function that creates and dispatches that action. In the Flux architecture, these functions are called action creator functions.

Creating an action creator

Let's create a new folder called `actions` in our project's `~/snapterest/source/actions` directory. Then, we'll create the `TweetActionCreators.js` file in it:

```
import AppDispatcher from '../dispatcher/AppDispatcher';

function receiveTweet(tweet) {
  const action = {
    type: 'receive_tweet',
    tweet
  };

  AppDispatcher.dispatch(action);
}

export { receiveTweet };
```

Our action creators will need a dispatcher to dispatch the actions. We will import `AppDispatcher` that we created previously:

```
import AppDispatcher from '../dispatcher/AppDispatcher';
```

Then, we will create our first action creator `receiveTweet()`:

```
function receiveTweet(tweet) {
  const action = {
    type: 'receive_tweet',
    tweet
  };

  AppDispatcher.dispatch(action);
}
```

The `receiveTweet()` function takes the `tweet` object as an argument, and creates the `action` object with a `type` property set to `receive_tweet`. It also adds the `tweet` object to our `action` object, and now every store will receive this `tweet` object.

Finally, the `receiveTweet()` action creator dispatches our `action` object by calling the `dispatch()` method on the `AppDispatcher` object:

```
AppDispatcher.dispatch(action);
```

The `dispatch()` method dispatches the `action` object to all the stores registered with the `AppDispatcher` dispatcher.

We then export our `receiveTweet` method:

```
export { receiveTweet };
```

So far, we've created `AppDispatcher` and `TweetActionCreators`. Next, let's create our first store.

Creating a store

As you learned earlier, stores manage data in your Flux architecture. They provide that data to the React components. We'll create a simple store that manages a new tweet that our application receives from Twitter.

Create a new folder called `stores` in our project's `~/snapterest/source/stores` directory. Then, create the `TweetStore.js` file in it:

```
import AppDispatcher from '../dispatcher/AppDispatcher';
import EventEmitter from 'events';

let tweet = null;

function setTweet(receivedTweet) {
  tweet = receivedTweet;
```

```
  }

  function emitChange() {
    TweetStore.emit('change');
  }

  const TweetStore = Object.assign({}, EventEmitter.prototype, {
    addChangeListener(callback) {
      this.on('change', callback);
    },

    removeChangeListener(callback) {
      this.removeListener('change', callback);
    },

    getTweet() {
      return tweet;
    }
  });

  function handleAction(action) {
    if (action.type === 'receive_tweet') {
      setTweet(action.tweet);
      emitChange();
    }
  }

  TweetStore.dispatchToken = AppDispatcher.register(handleAction);

  export default TweetStore;
```

The `TweetStore.js` file implements a simple store. We can break it into four logical parts:

- Importing dependency modules and creating private data and methods
- Creating the `TweetStore` object with public methods
- Creating an action handler and registering a store with a dispatcher
- Assigning `dispatchToken` to our `TweetStore` object and exporting it

In the first logical part of our store, we're simply importing the dependency modules that our store needs:

```
import AppDispatcher from '../dispatcher/AppDispatcher';
import EventEmitter from 'events';
```

Because our store will need to register with a dispatcher, we import the AppDispatcher module. Next, we import the EventEmitter class to be able to add and remove event listeners from our store:

```
import EventEmitter from 'events';
```

Once we import all the dependencies, we then define the data that our store manages:

```
let tweet = null;
```

The TweetStore object manages a simple tweet object that we initially set to null to identify that we didn't receive the new tweet yet.

Next, let's create the two private methods:

```
function setTweet(receivedTweet) {
   tweet = receivedTweet;
}

function emitChange() {
   TweetStore.emit('change');
}
```

The setTweet() function updates tweet with a receiveTweet object. The emitChange function emits the change event on the TweetStore object. These methods are private to the TweetStore module and they're not accessible outside of it.

The second logical part of the TweetStore.js file is creating the TweetStore object:

```
const TweetStore = Object.assign({}, EventEmitter.prototype, {
   addChangeListener(callback) {
     this.on('change', callback);
   },

   removeChangeListener(callback) {
     this.removeListener('change', callback);
   },

   getTweet() {
     return tweet;
   }
});
```

We want our store to be able to notify other parts of our application when its state has changed. We'll use events for this. Whenever our store updates its state, it emits the change event. Anyone interested in changes in the store's state can listen to this change event. They need to add their event listener function that our store will trigger on every change event. For this, our store defines the addChangeListener() method that adds the event listener, which listens to the change event, and the removeChangeListener() method that removes the change event listener. However, addChangeListener() and removeChangeListener() depend on methods provided by the EventEmitter.prototype object. So we need to copy the methods from the EventEmitter.prototype object to our TweetStore object. This is what the Object.assign() function does:

```
targetObject = Object.assign(
  targetObject,
  sourceObject1,
  sourceObject2
);
```

The Object.assign() copies the properties owned by sourceObject1 and sourceObject2 to targetObject and then it returns targetObject. In our case, sourceObject1 is EventEmitter.prototype, and sourceObject2 is an object literal that defines our store's methods:

```
{
  addChangeListener(callback) {
    this.on('change', callback);
  },

  removeChangeListener(callback) {
    this.removeListener('change', callback);
  },

  getTweet() {
    return tweet;
  }
}
```

The Object.assign() method returns targetObject with the properties copied from all the source objects. This is what our TweetStore object does.

Have you noticed that we define the getTweet() function as a method of our TweetStore object, whereas we don't do that with the setTweet() function. Why is that?

Later on, we'll export the TweetStore object, which means that all its properties will be available for other parts of our application to use. We want them to be able to get the data from TweetStore, but not to update that data directly by calling setTweet(). Instead, the only way to update data in any store is to create an action and dispatch it (using a dispatcher) to stores that have registered with that dispatcher. When the store gets that action, it can decide how to update its data.

This is a very important aspect of the Flux architecture. Stores are in full control of managing their data. They only allow other parts in our application to read that data, but never write to it directly. Only actions should mutate data in the stores.

The third logical part of the TweetStore.js file is creating an action handler and registering the store with a dispatcher.

First, we create the action handler function:

```
function handleAction(action) {
  if (action.type === 'receive_tweet') {
    setTweet(action.tweet);
    emitChange();
  }
}
```

The handleAction() function takes an action object as a parameter and checks its type property. In Flux, all stores get all the actions, but not all stores are interested in all the actions, so each store must decide what actions it's interested in. For this, a store must check for the action type. In our TweetStore store, we check whether the action type is receive_tweet, which means that our application has received a new tweet. If that's the case, then our TweetStore calls its private setTweet() function to update the tweet object with a new one that comes from the action object, that is, action.tweet. When the store changes its data, it needs to tell everyone who is interested in the data change. For this, it calls its private emitChange() function that emits the change event and triggers all the event listeners created by other parts in our application.

Our next task is to register the TweetStore store with a dispatcher. To register a store with a dispatcher, you need to call a dispatcher's register() method and pass the store's action handler function to it as a callback function. Whenever the dispatcher dispatches an action, it calls that callback function and passes the action object to it.

Let's take a look at our example:

```
TweetStore.dispatchToken = AppDispatcher.register(handleAction);
```

We call the `register()` method on the `AppDispatcher` object and pass the `handleAction` function as an argument. The `register()` method returns a token that identifies the `TweetStore` store. We save that token as a property of our `TweetStore` object.

The fourth logical part of the `TweetStore.js` file is exporting the `TweetStore` object:

```
export default TweetStore;
```

This is how you create a simple store. Now, since we have implemented our first action creator, dispatcher, and store, let's revisit the Flux architecture and take a look at a bigger picture of how it works:

1. The stores register themselves with a dispatcher.
2. Action creators create and dispatch actions to the stores via a dispatcher.
3. Stores check for relevant actions and change their data accordingly.
4. Stores notify everyone who is listening about the data change.

Well that makes sense, you may say, but what triggers action creators? Who is listening to store updates? These are very good questions to ask. And the answers are awaiting you in our next chapter.

Summary

In this chapter, you analyzed our React application's architecture. You learned the core concepts behind the Flux architecture, and you implemented a dispatcher, an action creator, and a store.

In the next chapter, we'll integrate them into our React application and get our architecture ready for the maintenance paradise.

11
Preparing Your React Application for Painless Maintenance with Flux

The reason why we decided to implement the Flux architecture in our React application is that we want to have a data flow that is easier to maintain. In the previous chapter, we implemented `AppDispatcher`, `TweetActionCreators`, and `TweetStore`. Let's quickly remember what they are used for:

- `TweetActionCreators`: This creates and dispatches the actions
- `AppDispatcher`: This dispatches all the actions to all stores
- `TweetStore`: This stores and manages the application data

The only missing parts in our data flow are as follows:

- Using `TweetActionCreators` to create the actions and start the data flowing
- Using `TweetStore` to get data

Here are a couple of important questions to ask: where in our application does the data flow start? What is our data? If we answer these questions, we will understand where to start refactoring our application to adapt the Flux architecture.

Snapterest allows users to receive and collect the latest tweets. The only data that our application is concerned with is tweets. So our data flow begins with receiving new tweets. What part of our application is responsible for receiving new tweets at the moment? You might remember that our `Stream` component has the following `componentDidMount()` method:

```
componentDidMount() {
    SnapkiteStreamClient.initializeStream(this.handleNewTweet);
}
```

Yes, currently, we initiate a stream of new tweets after we render the `Stream` component. Wait, you might ask, "Didn't we learn that React components should only be concerned with rendering the user interface?" You're correct. Unfortunately, at the moment, the `Stream` component is responsible for two different things:

- Rendering the `StreamTweet` component
- Initiating the data flow

Clearly, it's a potential maintenance issue in the future. Let's decouple these two different concerns with the help of Flux.

Decoupling concerns with Flux

First, we'll create a new utility module called `WebAPIUtils`. Create the `WebAPIUtils.js` file in the `~/snapterest/source/utils/` directory:

```
import SnapkiteStreamClient from 'snapkite-stream-client';
import { receiveTweet } from '../actions/TweetActionCreators';

function initializeStreamOfTweets() {
    SnapkiteStreamClient.initializeStream(receiveTweet);
}

export { initializeStreamOfTweets };
```

In this utility module, we first import the `SnapkiteStreamClient` library and `TweetActionCreators`. Then, we create the `initializeStreamOfTweets()` function that initializes a stream of new tweets, just like in the `componentDidMount()` method of the `Stream` component. Except with one key difference: whenever `SnapkiteStreamClient` receives a new tweet, it calls the `TweetActionCreators.receiveTweet` method that passes a new tweet to it as an argument:

```
SnapkiteStreamClient.initializeStream(receiveTweet);
```

Remember that the `receiveTweet` function expects to receive a `tweet` argument:

```
function receiveTweet(tweet) {
  // ... create and dispatch 'receive_tweet' action
}
```

This tweet will then be dispatched as a property of a new action object that the `receiveTweet()` function creates.

Then, the `WebAPIUtils` module exports our `initializeStreamOfTweets()` function.

Now we have a module with a method that initiates the data flow in our Flux architecture. Where should we import and call it? Since it's decoupled from the `Stream` component, and in fact, it doesn't depend on any React component at all, we can use it even before React renders anything. Let's use it in our `app.js` file:

```
import React from 'react';
import ReactDOM from 'react-dom';
import Application from './components/Application';
import { initializeStreamOfTweets } from './utils/WebAPIUtils';

initializeStreamOfTweets();

ReactDOM.render(
  <Application/>,
  document.getElementById('react-application')
);
```

As you can see, all that we need to do is to import and call the `initializeStreamOfTweets()` method:

```
import { initializeStreamOfTweets } from './utils/WebAPIUtils';

initializeStreamOfTweets();
```

We do this before calling React's `render()` method:

```
ReactDOM.render(
  <Application/>,
  document.getElementById('react-application')
);
```

In fact, as an experiment, you can remove the `ReactDOM.render()` line of code altogether, and put a log statement in the `TweetActionCreators.receiveTweet` function. For example, run the following code:

```
function receiveTweet(tweet) {

  console.log("I've received a new tweet and now will dispatch it
together with a new action.");

  const action = {
    type: 'receive_tweet',
    tweet
  };

  AppDispatcher.dispatch(action);
}
```

Now run the `npm start` command. Then, open `~/snapterest/build/index.html` in a web browser — you'll see the following text rendered on the page:

I am about to learn the essentials of React.js.

Now open JavaScript Console and you'll see this output:

[Snapkite Stream Client] Socket connected

I've received a new tweet and now will dispatch it together with a new action.

This log message will be printed out for each new tweet that our application receives. Even though we didn't render any React component, our Flux architecture is still there:

1. Our application receives a new tweet.
2. It creates and dispatches a new action.
3. No stores have registered with the dispatcher, so there is no one to receive the new action; hence, nothing is happening.

Now you can clearly see how React and Flux are two separate things that don't depend on each other at all.

However, we do want to render our React components. After all, we've put so much effort into creating them in the previous ten chapters! To do this, we need to put our `TweetStore` store into action. Can you guess where we should use it? Here's a hint: in a React component that needs a tweet to render itself — our good old `Stream` component.

Refactoring the Stream component

Now with the Flux architecture in place, we will rethink how our React components get data that they need to render. As you know, there are usually two sources of data for a React component:

- Calling another library, for example, calling the jQuery.ajax() method, or in our case, SnapkiteStreamClient.initializeStream()
- Receiving data from a parent React component via the props object

We want our React components to not use any external libraries to receive data. Instead, from now on, they will get that same data from stores. Keeping this plan in mind, let's refactor our Stream component.

Here is how it looks now:

```
import React from 'react';
import SnapkiteStreamClient from 'snapkite-stream-client';
import StreamTweet from './StreamTweet';
import Header from './Header';

class Stream extends React.Component {
  constructor() {
    super();

    this.state = {
      tweet: null
    };
  }

  componentDidMount() {
    SnapkiteStreamClient.initializeStream(this.handleNewTweet);
  }

  componentWillUnmount() {
    SnapkiteStreamClient.destroyStream();
  }

  handleNewTweet = tweet => {
    this.setState({
      tweet
    });
  }

  render() {
```

```
      const { tweet } = this.state;
      const { onAddTweetToCollection } = this.props;
      const headerText = "Waiting for public photos from Twitter...";

      if (tweet) {
        return (
          <StreamTweet
            tweet={tweet}
            onAddTweetToCollection={onAddTweetToCollection}
          />
        );
      }

      return (
        <Header text={headerText} />
      );
    }
  }

export default Stream;
```

First, let's get rid of the `componentDidMount()`, `componentWillUnmount()`, and `handleNewTweet()` methods and import the `TweetStore` store:

```
import React from 'react';
import SnapkiteStreamClient from 'snapkite-stream-client';
import StreamTweet from './StreamTweet';
import Header from './Header';
import TweetStore from '../stores/TweetStore';

class Stream extends React.Component {
  state = {
    tweet: null
  }

  render() {
    const { tweet } = this.state;
    const { onAddTweetToCollection } = this.props;
    const headerText =
    "Waiting for public photos from Twitter...";

    if (tweet) {
      return (
        <StreamTweet
          tweet={tweet}
```

```
                  onAddTweetToCollection={onAddTweetToCollection}
               />
            );
         }

      return (
         <Header text={headerText} />
      );
      }
   }

   export default Stream;
```

There is also no need to import the `snapkite-stream-client` module anymore.

Next, we need to change how the `Stream` component gets its initial tweet. Let's update its initial state:

```
state = {
   tweet: TweetStore.getTweet()
}
```

Code-wise, this might look like a small change, but it's a significant architectural improvement. We are now using the `getTweet()` method to get data from the `TweetStore` store. In the previous chapter, we discussed how stores expose the public methods in Flux in order to allow other parts of our application to get data from them. The `getTweet()` method is an example of one of these public methods, which are called *getters*.

You can get data from a store, but you can't set data on a store directly just like that. Stores have no public *setter* methods. They are purposely designed with this limitation in mind so that when you write your application with Flux, your data can only flow in one direction. This will benefit you hugely down the road when you'll need to maintain your Flux application.

Now we know how to get our initial tweet, but how do we get all the other new tweets that will arrive later? We can create a timer and call `TweetStore.getTweet()` repeatedly; however, this is not the best solution because it assumes that we don't know when `TweetStore` updates its tweet with a new one. However, we do know that.

How? Remember that in the previous chapter, we implemented the following public methods on the TweetStore object, that is, the addChangeListener() method:

```
addChangeListener(callback) {
  this.on('change', callback);
}
```

We implemented the removeChangeListener() method as well:

```
removeChangeListener(callback) {
  this.removeListener('change', callback);
}
```

That's right. We can ask TweetStore to tell us when it changes its data. For this, we need to call its addChangeListener() method and pass it a callback function that TweetStore will call for each new tweet. The question is that in our Stream component, where do we call the TweetStore.addChangeListener() method?

Since we need to add the change event listener to TweetStore only once per component's lifecycle, it makes componentDidMount() a perfect candidate. Add the following componentDidMount() method to the Stream component:

```
componentDidMount() {
  TweetStore.addChangeListener(this.onTweetChange);
}
```

Here, we add our own change event listener, this.onTweetChange, to TweetStore. Now when TweetStore changes its data, it will trigger our this.onTweetChange method. We will create this method shortly.

Don't forget that we need to remove any event listeners before we unmount our React component. To do this, add the following componentWillUnmount() method to the Stream component:

```
componentWillUnmount() {
  TweetStore.removeChangeListener(this.onTweetChange);
}
```

Removing an event listener is very similar to adding it. We call the TweetStore.removeChangeListener() method and pass our this.onTweetChange method as an argument.

Now, it's time to create the `onTweetChange` method in our `Stream` component:

```
onTweetChange = () => {
  this.setState({
    tweet: TweetStore.getTweet()
  });
}
```

As you can see, it updates the component's state with a new tweet stored in `TweetStore` using the `TweetStore.getTweet()` method.

There is one final change that we need to make in our `Stream` component. Later in this chapter, you'll learn that our `StreamTweet` component doesn't need the `handleAddTweetToCollection()` callback function anymore; therefore, in this component, we're going to change the following code snippet:

```
return (
  <StreamTweet
    tweet={tweet}
    onAddTweetToCollection={onAddTweetToCollection}
  />
);
```

Replace it with the following code:

```
return (<StreamTweet tweet={tweet} />);
```

Now let's take a look at our newly refactored `Stream` component:

```
import React from 'react';
import StreamTweet from './StreamTweet';
import Header from './Header';
import TweetStore from '../stores/TweetStore';

class Stream extends React.Component {
  state = {
    tweet: TweetStore.getTweet()
  }

  componentDidMount() {
    TweetStore.addChangeListener(this.onTweetChange);
  }

  componentWillUnmount() {
```

```
      TweetStore.removeChangeListener(this.onTweetChange);
    }

    onTweetChange = () => {
      this.setState({
        tweet: TweetStore.getTweet()
      });
    }

    render() {
      const { tweet } = this.state;
      const { onAddTweetToCollection } = this.props;
      const headerText =
      "Waiting for public photos from Twitter...";

      if (tweet) {
        return (<StreamTweet tweet={tweet}/>);
      }

      return (<Header text={headerText}/>);
    }
  }

  export default Stream;
```

Let's recap to see how our `Stream` component always has the latest tweet:

1. We set the component's initial tweet to the latest tweet that we get from `TweetStore` using the `getTweet()` method.

2. Then, we listen to changes in `TweetStore`.

3. When `TweetStore` changes its tweet, we update the component's state to the latest tweet that we get from `TweetStore` using the `getTweet()` method.

4. When the component is about to unmount, we stop listening to the changes in `TweetStore`.

This is how a React component interacts with a Flux store.

Before we move on to make the rest of our application Flux-strong, let's take a look at our current data flow:

- `app.js`: This receives the new tweets and calls `TweetActionCreators` for each tweet

- `TweetActionCreators`: This creates and dispatches a new action with a new tweet

- AppDispatcher: This dispatches all the actions to all stores
- TweetStore: This registers with a dispatcher and emits the change event on every new action received from a dispatcher
- Stream: This listens to changes in TweetStore, gets a new tweet from TweetStore, updates the state with a new tweet, and re-renders

Can you see how we can now scale the number of React components, action creators, and stores, and still be able to maintain Snapterest? With Flux, it will always be a one-way data flow. It will be the same mental model regardless of how many new features we'll implement. We will hugely benefit in the long run, when we'll need to maintain our app.

Did I mention that we're going to adapt Flux in our application even more? Next, let's do exactly that.

Creating CollectionStore

Not only does Snapterest store the latest tweet, but it also stores a collection of tweets that users create. Let's refactor this feature with Flux.

First, let's create a collection store. Navigate to the ~/snapterest/source/stores/ directory and create the CollectionStore.js file:

```
import AppDispatcher from '../dispatcher/AppDispatcher';
import { EventEmitter } from 'events';

const CHANGE_EVENT = 'change';

let collectionTweets = {};
let collectionName = 'new';

function addTweetToCollection(tweet) {
  collectionTweets[tweet.id] = tweet;
}

function removeTweetFromCollection(tweetId) {
  delete collectionTweets[tweetId];
}

function removeAllTweetsFromCollection() {
  collectionTweets = {};
}
```

```
function setCollectionName(name) {
  collectionName = name;
}


function emitChange() {
  CollectionStore.emit(CHANGE_EVENT);
}


const CollectionStore = Object.assign(
  {}, EventEmitter.prototype, {
  addChangeListener(callback) {
    this.on(CHANGE_EVENT, callback);
  },

  removeChangeListener(callback) {
    this.removeListener(CHANGE_EVENT, callback);
  },

  getCollectionTweets() {
    return collectionTweets;
  },

  getCollectionName() {
    return collectionName;
  }
}
);


function handleAction(action) {

  switch (action.type) {
    case 'add_tweet_to_collection':
      addTweetToCollection(action.tweet);
      emitChange();
      break;

    case 'remove_tweet_from_collection':
      removeTweetFromCollection(action.tweetId);
      emitChange();
      break;

    case 'remove_all_tweets_from_collection':
      removeAllTweetsFromCollection();
      emitChange();
```

```
    break;

  case 'set_collection_name':
    setCollectionName(action.collectionName);
    emitChange();
    break;

  default: // ... do nothing

  }
}


CollectionStore.dispatchToken =
AppDispatcher.register(handleAction);

export default CollectionStore;
```

The `CollectionStore` is a bigger store, but it has the same structure as `TweetStore`.

First, we import the dependencies and assign a `change` event name to the CHANGE_
EVENT variable:

```
import AppDispatcher from '../dispatcher/AppDispatcher';
import { EventEmitter } from 'events';

const CHANGE_EVENT = 'change';
```

Then, we define our data and the four private methods that mutate this data:

```
let collectionTweets = {};
let collectionName = 'new';

function addTweetToCollection(tweet) {
  collectionTweets[tweet.id] = tweet;
}

function removeTweetFromCollection(tweetId) {
  delete collectionTweets[tweetId];
}

function removeAllTweetsFromCollection() {
  collectionTweets = {};
}

function setCollectionName(name) {
  collectionName = name;
}
```

As you can see, we store a collection of tweets in an object that is initially empty, and we also store the collection name that is initially set to `new`. Then, we create three private functions that mutate `collectionTweets`:

- `addTweetToCollection()`: As the name suggests, it adds the `tweet` object to the `collectionTweets` object
- `removeTweetFromCollection()`: This removes the `tweet` object from the `collectionTweets` object
- `removeAllTweetsFromCollection()`: This removes all the `tweet` objects from `collectionTweets` by setting it to an empty object

Then, we define one private function that mutates `collectionName` called `setCollectionName`, which changes the existing collection name to a new one.

These functions are regarded as private because they are not accessible outside the `CollectionStore` module; for example, you *can't* access them like that in any other module:

```
CollectionStore.setCollectionName('impossible');
```

As we discussed earlier, this is done on purpose to enforce a one-way data flow in your application.

We create the `emitChange()` method that emits the `change` event.

Then, we create the `CollectionStore` object:

```
const CollectionStore = Object.assign(
  {}, EventEmitter.prototype, {
  addChangeListener(callback) {
    this.on(CHANGE_EVENT, callback);
  },

  removeChangeListener(callback) {
    this.removeListener(CHANGE_EVENT, callback);
  },

  getCollectionTweets() {
    return collectionTweets;
  },

  getCollectionName() {
    return collectionName;
  }
});
```

This is very similar to the `TweetStore` object, except for two methods:

- `getCollectionTweets()`: This returns a collection of tweets
- `getCollectionName()`: This returns the collection name

These methods are accessible outside the `CollectionStore.js` file and should be used in React components to get data from `CollectionStore`.

Then, we create the `handleAction()` function:

```
function handleAction(action) {
  switch (action.type) {

    case 'add_tweet_to_collection':
      addTweetToCollection(action.tweet);
      emitChange();
      break;

    case 'remove_tweet_from_collection':
      removeTweetFromCollection(action.tweetId);
      emitChange();
      break;

    case 'remove_all_tweets_from_collection':
      removeAllTweetsFromCollection();
      emitChange();
      break;

    case 'set_collection_name':
      setCollectionName(action.collectionName);
      emitChange();
      break;

    default: // ... do nothing

  }
}
```

This function handles the actions that are dispatched by `AppDispatcher`, but unlike `TweetStore` in our `CollectionStore` module, we can handle more than one action. In fact, we can handle the four actions that are related to the collection of tweets:

- `add_tweet_to_collection`: This adds a tweet to a collection
- `remove_tweet_from_collection`: This removes a tweet from a collection
- `remove_all_tweets_from_collection`: This removes all the tweets from a collection
- `set_collection_name`: This sets a collection name

Remember that all the stores receive all the actions, so `CollectionStore` will receive the `receive_tweet` action as well, but we simply ignore it in this store, just like `TweetStore` ignores `add_tweet_to_collection`, `remove_tweet_from_collection`, `remove_all_tweets_from_collection`, and `set_collection_name`.

Then, we register the `handleAction` callback with `AppDispatcher`, and save `dispatchToken` in the `CollectionStore` object:

```
CollectionStore.dispatchToken =
AppDispatcher.register(handleAction);
```

Finally, we export `CollectionStore` as a module:

```
export default CollectionStore;
```

Now since we have the collection store ready, let's create action creator functions next.

Creating CollectionActionCreators

Navigate to `~/snapterest/source/actions/` and create the `CollectionActionCreators.js` file:

```
import AppDispatcher from '../dispatcher/AppDispatcher';

function addTweetToCollection(tweet) {
  const action = {
    type: 'add_tweet_to_collection',
    tweet
  };

  AppDispatcher.dispatch(action);
}

function removeTweetFromCollection(tweetId) {
```

```
  const action = {
    type: 'remove_tweet_from_collection',
    tweetId
  };

  AppDispatcher.dispatch(action);
}

function removeAllTweetsFromCollection() {
  const action = {
    type: 'remove_all_tweets_from_collection'
  };

  AppDispatcher.dispatch(action);
}

function setCollectionName(collectionName) {
  const action = {
    type: 'set_collection_name',
    collectionName
  };

  AppDispatcher.dispatch(action);
}

export default {
  addTweetToCollection,
  removeTweetFromCollection,
  removeAllTweetsFromCollection,
  setCollectionName
};
```

For each action that we handle in `CollectionStore`, we have an action creator function:

- `addTweetToCollection()`: This creates and dispatches the `add_tweet_to_collection` action with a new tweet

- `removeTweetFromCollection()`: This creates and dispatches the `remove_tweet_from_collection` action with the ID of the tweet that must be removed from the collection

- `removeAllTweetsFromCollection()`: This creates and dispatches the `remove_all_tweets_from_collection` action

- `setCollectionName()`: This creates and dispatches the `set_collection_name` action with a new collection name

Now when we've created both the `CollectionStore` and `CollectionActionCreators` modules, we can start refactoring our React components to adopt the Flux architecture.

Refactoring the Application component

Where do we start refactoring our React components? Let's start with our topmost React component in our components hierarchy, `Application`.

At the moment, our `Application` component stores and manages the collection of tweets. Let's remove this functionality as it's now managed by the collection store.

Remove the `constructor()`, `addTweetToCollection()`, `removeTweetFromCollection()`, and `removeAllTweetsFromCollection()` methods from the `Application` component:

```
import React from 'react';
import Stream from './Stream';
import Collection from './Collection';

class Application extends React.Component {
  render() {
    const {
      collectionTweets
    } = this.state;

    return (
      <div className="container-fluid">
        <div className="row">
          <div className="col-md-4 text-center">
            <Stream onAddTweetToCollection=
            {this.addTweetToCollection}/>

          </div>
          <div className="col-md-8">
            <Collection
              tweets={collectionTweets}
              onRemoveTweetFromCollection=
              {this.removeTweetFromCollection}
              onRemoveAllTweetsFromCollection=
              {this.removeAllTweetsFromCollection}
            />
          </div>
        </div>
      </div>
```

```
        </div>
      );
    }
}

export default Application;
```

Now the `Application` component has only the `render()` method that renders the `Stream` and `Collection` components. Since it doesn't manage the collection of tweets anymore, we don't need to pass any properties to the `Stream` and `Collection` components as well.

Update the `Application` component's `render()` function, as follows:

```
render() {
  return (
    <div className="container-fluid">
      <div className="row">
        <div className="col-md-4 text-center">
          <Stream/>
        </div>
        <div className="col-md-8">
          <Collection/>
        </div>
      </div>

    </div>
  );
}
```

The adoption of the Flux architecture allows the `Stream` component to manage the latest tweet and the `Collection` component to manage the collection of tweets, whereas the `Application` component doesn't need to manage anything anymore, so it becomes a container component that wraps the `Stream` and `Collection` components in the additional HTML markup.

In fact, you might have noticed that our current version of `Application` component is a good candidate to become a functional React component:

```
import React from 'react';
import Stream from './Stream';
import Collection from './Collection';

const Application = () =>(
  <div className="container-fluid">
    <div className="row">
```

```
          <div className="col-md-4 text-center">
            <Stream />
          </div>
          <div className="col-md-8">
            <Collection />
          </div>
        </div>
      </div>
    );

    export default Application;
```

Our `Application` component is now much simpler and its markup looks much cleaner. This improves the component's maintainability. Well done!

Refactoring the Collection component

Next, let's refactor our `Collection` component. Replace the existing `Collection` component with the following:

```
import React, { Component } from 'react';
import ReactDOMServer from 'react-dom/server';
import CollectionControls from './CollectionControls';
import TweetList from './TweetList';
import Header from './Header';
import CollectionUtils from '../utils/CollectionUtils';
import CollectionStore from '../stores/CollectionStore';

class Collection extends Component {
  state = {
    collectionTweets: CollectionStore.getCollectionTweets()
  }

  componentDidMount() {
    CollectionStore.addChangeListener(this.onCollectionChange);
  }

  componentWillUnmount() {
    CollectionStore.removeChangeListener(this.onCollectionChange);
  }

  onCollectionChange = () => {
    this.setState({
```

```
      collectionTweets: CollectionStore.getCollectionTweets()
    });
  }

  createHtmlMarkupStringOfTweetList() {
    const htmlString = ReactDOMServer.renderToStaticMarkup(
      <TweetList tweets={this.state.collectionTweets}/>
    );

    const htmlMarkup = {
      html: htmlString
    };

    return JSON.stringify(htmlMarkup);
  }

  render() {
    const { collectionTweets } = this.state;
    const numberOfTweetsInCollection = CollectionUtils
      .getNumberOfTweetsInCollection(collectionTweets);
    let htmlMarkup;

    if (numberOfTweetsInCollection > 0) {
      htmlMarkup = this.createHtmlMarkupStringOfTweetList();

      return (
        <div>
          <CollectionControls
            numberOfTweetsInCollection=
            {numberOfTweetsInCollection}
            htmlMarkup={htmlMarkup}
          />

          <TweetList tweets={collectionTweets} />
        </div>
      );
    }

    return (<Header text="Your collection is empty" />);
  }
}

export default Collection;
```

What did we change here? A few things. First, we imported the two new modules:

```
import CollectionUtils from '../utils/CollectionUtils';
import CollectionStore from '../stores/CollectionStore';
```

We created the `CollectionUtils` module in *Chapter 9, Testing Your React Application with Jest*, and in this chapter, we're using it. `CollectionStore` is where we get our data from.

Next, you should be able to spot the familiar pattern of the four methods:

- In the initial state, we set the collection of tweets to what is stored in `CollectionStore` at that moment. As you may recall that `CollectionStore` provides the `getCollectionTweets()` method to get the data from it.

- In the `componentDidMount()` method, we add the `change` event listener, `this.onCollectionChange` to `CollectionStore`. Whenever the collection of tweets is updated, `CollectionStore` will call our `this. onCollectionChange` callback function to notify the `Collection` component of that change.

- In the `componentWillUnmount()` method, we remove the `change` event listener that we added to the `componentDidMount()` method.

- In the `onCollectionChange()` method, we set the component's state to whatever is stored in `CollectionStore` at that moment in time. Updating the component's state triggers a re-render.

The `Collection` component's `render()` method is now simpler and cleaner:

```
render() {
  const { collectionTweets } = this.state;
  const numberOfTweetsInCollection = CollectionUtils
    .getNumberOfTweetsInCollection(collectionTweets);
  let htmlMarkup;

  if (numberOfTweetsInCollection > 0) {
    htmlMarkup = this.createHtmlMarkupStringOfTweetList();

    return (
      <div>
        <CollectionControls
          numberOfTweetsInCollection={numberOfTweetsInCollection}
          htmlMarkup={htmlMarkup}
        />

        <TweetList tweets={collectionTweets}/>
```

```
      </div>
    );
  }

  return (<Header text="Your collection is empty"/>);
}
```

We use the `CollectionUtils` module to get a number of tweets in the collection, and we pass fewer properties to the child components: `CollectionControls` and `TweetList`.

Refactoring the CollectionControls component

The `CollectionControls` component gets some major improvements as well. Let's take a look at the refactored version first and then discuss what was updated and why:

```
import React, { Component } from 'react';
import Header from './Header';
import Button from './Button';
import CollectionRenameForm from './CollectionRenameForm';
import CollectionExportForm from './CollectionExportForm';
import CollectionActionCreators from
'../actions/CollectionActionCreators';
import CollectionStore from '../stores/CollectionStore';

class CollectionControls extends Component {
  state = {
    isEditingName: false
  }

  getHeaderText = () => {
    const { numberOfTweetsInCollection } = this.props;
    let text = numberOfTweetsInCollection;
    const name = CollectionStore.getCollectionName();

    if (numberOfTweetsInCollection === 1) {
      text = `${text} tweet in your`;
    } else {
      text = `${text} tweets in your`;
    }

    return (
```

```
      <span>
        {text} <strong>{name}</strong> collection
      </span>
    );
  }

  toggleEditCollectionName = () => {
    this.setState(prevState => ({
      isEditingName: !prevState.isEditingName
    }));
  }

  removeAllTweetsFromCollection = () => {
    CollectionActionCreators.removeAllTweetsFromCollection();
  }

  render() {
    const { name, isEditingName } = this.state;
    const onRemoveAllTweetsFromCollection =
    this.removeAllTweetsFromCollection;
    const { htmlMarkup } = this.props;

    if (isEditingName) {
      return (
        <CollectionRenameForm
          name={name}
          onCancelCollectionNameChange=
          {this.toggleEditCollectionName}
        />
      );
    }

    return (
      <div>
        <Header text={this.getHeaderText()} />

        <Button
          label="Rename collection"
          handleClick={this.toggleEditCollectionName}
        />

        <Button
          label="Empty collection"
          handleClick={onRemoveAllTweetsFromCollection}
```

```
        />

        <CollectionExportForm htmlMarkup={htmlMarkup} />
      </div>
    );
  }
}

export default CollectionControls;
```

First, we import the two additional modules:

```
import CollectionActionCreators from
'../actions/CollectionActionCreators';
import CollectionStore from '../stores/CollectionStore';
```

Notice that we don't manage the collection name in this component anymore. Instead, we get it from our `CollectionStore` module:

```
const name = CollectionStore.getCollectionName();
```

Then, we make one of the key changes. We replace the `setCollectionName()` method with a new one, `removeAllTweetsFromCollection()`:

```
removeAllTweetsFromCollection - () => {
  CollectionActionCreators.removeAllTweetsFromCollection();
}
```

The `removeAllTweetsFromCollection()` method is called when a user clicks on the `Empty Collection` button. This user action triggers the `removeAllTweetsFromCollection()` action creator function that creates and dispatches the action to stores. In turn, `CollectionStore` removes all the tweets from the collection and emits the `change` event.

Next, let's refactor our `CollectionRenameForm` component.

Refactoring the CollectionRenameForm component

`CollectionRenameForm` is a controlled form component. This means that its input value is stored in the component's state, and the only way to update that value is to update the component's state. It has the initial value that it should get from `CollectionStore`, so let's make that happen.

First, import the `CollectionActionCreators` and `CollectionStore` modules:

```
import CollectionActionCreators from
'../actions/CollectionActionCreators';
import CollectionStore from '../stores/CollectionStore';
```

Now, we need to remove its existing `constructor()` method:

```
constructor(props) {
  super(props);

  const { name } = props;

  this.state = {
    inputValue: name
  };
}
```

Replace the preceding code with the following:

```
state = {
  inputValue: CollectionStore.getCollectionName()
}
```

As you can see, the only difference is that now we get the initial `inputValue` from `CollectionStore`.

Next, let's update the `handleFormSubmit()` method:

```
handleFormSubmit = event => {
  event.preventDefault();

  const { onChangeCollectionName } = this.props;
  const { inputValue: collectionName } = this.state;

  onChangeCollectionName(collectionName);
}
```

Update the preceding code with the following:

```
handleFormSubmit = event => {
  event.preventDefault();

  const { onCancelCollectionNameChange } = this.props;
```

```
    const { inputValue: collectionName } = this.state;

    CollectionActionCreators.setCollectionName(collectionName);

    onCancelCollectionNameChange();
}
```

The important difference here is that when a user submits a form, we will create a new action that sets a new name in our collection store:

```
CollectionActionCreators.setCollectionName(collectionName);
```

Finally, we need to change the source of the collection name in the `handleFormCancel()` method:

```
handleFormCancel = event => {
    event.preventDefault();

    const {
        name: collectionName,
        onCancelCollectionNameChange
    } = this.props;

    this.setInputValue(collectionName);
    onCancelCollectionNameChange();
}
```

Change the preceding code with the following code:

```
handleFormCancel = event => {
    event.preventDefault();

    const {
        onCancelCollectionNameChange
    } = this.props;

    const collectionName = CollectionStore.getCollectionName();

    this.setInputValue(collectionName);
    onCancelCollectionNameChange();
}
```

Once again, we get the collection name from a collection store:

```
const collectionName = CollectionStore.getCollectionName();
```

This is all that we need to change in the `CollectionRenameForm` component. Let's refactor the `TweetList` component next.

Refactoring the TweetList component

The `TweetList` component renders a list of tweets. Each tweet is a `Tweet` component that a user can click on to remove it from a collection. Does it sound to you like it could make use of `CollectionActionCreators`?

That's right. Let's add the `CollectionActionCreators` module to it:

```
import CollectionActionCreators from
'../actions/CollectionActionCreators';
```

Then, we'll create the `removeTweetFromCollection()` callback function that will be called when a user clicks on a tweet image:

```
removeTweetFromCollection = tweet => {
    CollectionActionCreators.removeTweetFromCollection(tweet.id);
}
```

As you can see, it creates a new action using the `removeTweetFromCollection()` function by passing the tweet ID as an argument to it.

Finally, we need to make sure that `removeTweetFromCollection()` is actually called. In the `getTweetElement()` method, find the following line:

```
const { tweets, onRemoveTweetFromCollection } = this.props;
```

Now replace it with the following code:

```
const { tweets } = this.props;
const onRemoveTweetFromCollection =
this.removeTweetFromCollection;
```

We're all done with this component. `StreamTweet` is next in our refactoring journey.

Refactoring the StreamTweet component

StreamTweet renders a tweet image that a user can click on to add it to a collection of tweets. You might have already guessed that we're going to create and dispatch a new action when a user clicks on that tweet image.

First, import the CollectionActionCreators module to the StreamTweet component:

```
import CollectionActionCreators from
  '../actions/CollectionActionCreators';
```

Then, add a new addTweetToCollection() method to it:

```
addTweetToCollection = tweet => {
  CollectionActionCreators.addTweetToCollection(tweet);
}
```

The addTweetToCollection() callback function should be invoked when a user clicks on a tweet image. Let's take a look at this line in the render() method:

```
<Tweet
  tweet={tweet}
  onImageClick={onAddTweetToCollection}
/>
```

Replace the preceding code with the following line of code:

```
<Tweet
  tweet={tweet}
  onImageClick={this.addTweetToCollection}
/>
```

Finally, we need to replace the following line:

```
const { tweet, onAddTweetToCollection } = this.props;
```

Use this one instead:

```
const { tweet } = this.props;
```

The StreamTweet component is now done.

Building and going beyond

That's all the effort that is needed to integrate the Flux architecture into our React application. If you compare your React application without Flux and with Flux, you'll quickly see how much easier it is to understand how your application works when Flux is part of it. You can learn more about Flux at `https://facebook. github.io/flux/`.

I think it's a good time to check that everything is in perfect working order. Let's build and run Snapterest!

Navigate to `~/snapterest` and run the following command in your Terminal window:

```
npm start
```

Make sure that you're running the Snapkite Engine application that we have installed and configured in *Chapter 2, Installing Powerful Tools for Your Project*. Now open the `~/snapterest/build/index.html` file in your web browser. You should see new tweets appearing on the left-hand side, one at a time. Click on a tweet to add it to a collection that appears on the right-hand side.

Does it work? Check JavaScript Console for any errors. No errors?

Congratulations on integrating the Flux architecture into our React application!

Summary

In this chapter, we completed refactoring our application to use the Flux architecture. You learned what it takes to combine React with Flux and what advantages Flux has to offer.

In the next chapter, we'll simplify our application's architecture further with the Redux library.

12
Refining Your Flux Apps with Redux

The preceding chapter walked you through the implementation of a full-fledged React application built on top of a Flux architecture. In this chapter, you'll make some modifications to this app so that it uses the Redux library to implement the Flux architecture. Here's how this chapter is organized:

- A brief overview of Redux
- Implementing reducer functions that control state
- Building Redux action creators
- Connecting components to Redux stores
- The Redux entry point into your application's state

Why Redux?

Before we get started with refactoring your application, we'll spend a couple of minutes looking at Redux at a high level. Just enough to whet your appetite. Ready?

One store to rule them all

The first major difference between traditional Flux applications and Redux is that, with Redux, you only have one store. A traditional Flux architecture might only call for one store as well, but it might have several of them. You would think that having multiple stores could actually simplify the architecture since you could separate states by different sections of the application. Indeed, this is a good tactic, but it doesn't necessarily hold up in practice. Creating more than one store can lead to confusion. Stores are moving parts in your architecture; if you have more of them, there's more potential for something to go wrong.

Redux removes this factor by allowing only one store. You might think that this would lead to a monolithic data structure that's difficult for various application features to use. This isn't the case, because you're free to structure your store any way you please.

Fewer moving parts

By only allowing one store, Redux takes moving parts out of the picture. Another place where Redux simplifies your architecture is in removing the need for a dedicated dispatcher. In traditional Flux architectures, the dispatcher is a distinct component that sends messages to stores. Since there's only one store in Redux architectures, you can just dispatch actions directly to the store. In other words, the store is the dispatcher.

The final place that Redux reduces the number of moving parts in your code is in event listeners. In traditional Flux applications, you have to manually subscribe and unsubscribe from store events in order to wire everything up correctly. This is a distraction when you can have a library handle the wiring work for you. This is something that Redux does well.

Uses the best parts of Flux

Redux is not Flux, in the traditional sense. Flux has a specification and a library that implements it. Redux is not this. As mentioned in the preceding section, Redux is a simplification of Flux. It keeps all of the Flux concepts that lead to sound application architectures while ignoring the tedious bits that can make Flux difficult to implement and ultimately difficult to adopt.

Controlling state with reducers

The flagship concept of Redux is that, state is controlled by reducer functions. In this section, we'll get you caught up on what reducers are, followed by the implementation of reducer functions in your Snapterest app.

What are reducers?

Reducers are functions that take a data collection, such as an object or an array, and return a new collection. The returned collection can have the same data in it, or it can have completely different data than the initial collection. In Redux applications, reducer functions take a slice of state, and return a new slice of state. That's it! You've just learned the crux of the Redux architecture. Now let's see reducer functions in action.

Reducer functions in Redux applications can be separated into modules that represent the part of the application state they work with. We'll look at the collection reducers, followed by the tweet reducers of the Snapterest app.

Collection reducers

Now let's walk through the collection reducer function that changes part of the application state. First, let's take a look at the function in its entirety:

```
const collectionReducer = (
  state = initialState,
  action
) => {
  let tweet;
  let collectionTweets;

  switch (action.type) {
    case 'add_tweet_to_collection':
      tweet = {};
      tweet[action.tweet.id] = action.tweet;

      return {
        ...state,
        collectionTweets: {
          ...state.collectionTweets,
          ...tweet
        }
      };

    case 'remove_tweet_from_collection':
      collectionTweets = { ...state.collectionTweets };
      delete collectionTweets[action.tweetId];

      return {
        ...state,
        collectionTweets
      };

    case 'remove_all_tweets_from_collection':
      collectionTweets = {};

      return {
        ...state,
        collectionTweets
```

```
        };

    case 'set_collection_name':
      return {
        ...state,
        collectionName: state.editingName,
        isEditingName: false
      };

    case 'toggle_is_editing_name':
      return {
        ...state,
        isEditingName: !state.isEditingName
      };

    case 'set_editing_name':
      return {
        ...state,
        editingName: action.editingName
      };

    default:
      return state;
  }
};
```

As you can see, the new state that's returned is based on the action that was dispatched. The action name is supplied to this function as an argument. Now let's walk through the different scenarios of this reducer.

Adding tweets to collections

Let's take a look at the add_tweet_to_collection action:

```
case 'add_tweet_to_collection':
  tweet = {};
  tweet[action.tweet.id] = action.tweet;

  return {
    ...state,
    collectionTweets: {
      ...state.collectionTweets,
      ...tweet
    }
  };
```

The switch statement detects that action type is add_tweet_to_collection. The action also has a tweet property that contains the actual tweet to add. The tweet variable is used here to build an object with the tweet ID as the key, and tweet as the value. This is the format that the collectionTweets object is expecting.

Then we return the new state. It's important to remember that this should always be a new object, not a reference to some other object. This is how you avoid unintended side-effects in Redux applications. Thankfully, we can use the object spread operator to simplify this task.

Removing tweets from collections

Removing a tweet from the collectionTweets object means that we have to delete the key which has the tweet ID to be deleted. Let's see how this is done:

```
case 'remove_tweet_from_collection':
  collectionTweets = { ...state.collectionTweets };
  delete collectionTweets[action.tweetId];

  return {
    ...state,
    collectionTweets
  };
```

Notice how we're assigning a new object to the collectionTweets variable? Once again, the spread operator comes in handy here to avoid extra syntax. The reason we're doing it this way is so that the reducer always returns a new reference. Once we delete the tweet from our collectionTweets object, we can return the new state object that includes collectionTweets as a property.

The other tweet removal action is remove_all_tweets_from_collection. Here's what it looks like:

```
case 'remove_all_tweets_from_collection':
  collectionTweets = {};

  return {
    ...state,
    collectionTweets
  };
```

Removing all tweets means that we can just replace the collectionTweets value with a new empty object.

Setting the collection name

When a collection of tweets is renamed, we have to update the Redux store. This is done by getting `editingName` from the state when the `set_collection_name` action is dispatched:

```
case 'set_collection_name':
  return {
    ...state,
    collectionName: state.editingName,
    isEditingName: false
  };
```

You can see that the `collectionName` value is set to `editingName`, and `isEditingName` is set to `false`. This is meant to indicate that since the value has been set, we know that the user is no longer editing the name.

Editing collection names

You just saw how to set the collection name once the user saves their changes. However, there's more to editing text when it comes to tracking state in Redux stores. First, we have to enable the text to be edited in the first place; this gives the user some sort of visual cue:

```
case 'toggle_is_editing_name':
  return {
    ...state,
    isEditingName: !state.isEditingName
  };
```

Then, there's the text that the user is actively typing in the text input. This has to go somewhere in the store too:

```
case 'set_editing_name':
  return {
    ...state,
    editingName: action.editingName
  };
```

Not only will this cause the appropriate React components to re-render, but it also means that we have the text stored in the state, ready to go when the user is finished editing.

Tweet reducers

There is only one action that the tweet reducer needs to handle, but this doesn't mean that we shouldn't have the tweet reducer in its own module in anticipation of future actions for tweets. For now, let's just focus on what our app currently does.

Receiving tweets

Let's take a look at the tweet reducer code that handles the `receive_tweet` action:

```
const tweetReducer = (state = null, action) => {
  switch(action.type) {
    case 'receive_tweet':
      return action.tweet;
    default:
      return state;
  }
};
```

This reducer is pretty straightforward. The `action.tweet` value is returned as the new state when the `receive_tweet` action is dispatched. Since this is a small reducer function, it might be a good place to point out some things that are common to all reducer functions.

The first argument that is passed to a reducer function is the old state. This argument has a default value because the first time the reducer is called, there is no state and this value is used to initialize it. In this case, the default state is null.

The second thing to point out about reducers is that they always return a new state when called. Even if it doesn't produce any new state, a reducer function needs to return the old state. Redux will set the new state to whatever is returned by the reducer, even if you return undefined. This is why it's a good idea to have a `default` label in your `switch` statements.

Simplified action creators

In Redux, action creator functions are simpler than their traditional Flux counterparts. The main difference is that Redux action creator functions just return the action data. In traditional Flux, the action creators are also responsible for calling the dispatcher. Let's take a look at the Redux action creator functions for Snapterest:

```
export const addTweetToCollection = tweet => ({
  type: 'add_tweet_to_collection',
  tweet
```

```
  });

  export const removeTweetFromCollection = tweetId => ({
    type: 'remove_tweet_from_collection',
    tweetId
  });

  export const removeAllTweetsFromCollection = () => ({
    type: 'remove_all_tweets_from_collection'
  });

  export const setCollectionName = collectionName => ({
    type: 'set_collection_name',
    collectionName
  });

  export const toggleIsEditingName = () => ({
    type: 'toggle_is_editing_name'
  });

  export const setEditingName = editingName => ({
    type: 'set_editing_name',
    editingName
  });

  export const receiveTweet = tweet => ({
    type: 'receive_tweet',
    tweet
  });
```

As you can see, these functions return action objects that can then be
dispatched—they don't actually call the dispatcher. You'll see why this is the case
when we start connecting our React components to the Redux store. The main
responsibility of action creator functions in a Redux app is to make sure that an
object with the correct `type` property is returned, along with properties that are
relevant to the action. For example, the `addTweetToCollection()` action creator
accepts a tweet parameter, which is then passed to the action by returning it as a
property of the returned object.

Connecting components to an application state

So far, we have the reducer functions that handle creating a new application state, and the action creator functions that trigger our reducer functions. We still need to connect our React components to the Redux store. In this section, you'll learn how to use the `connect()` function to create a new version of your component that's connected to the Redux store.

Mapping state and action creators to props

The idea with Redux and React integration is that you tell Redux to wrap your component with a stateful component that has its state set when the Redux store changes. All we have to do is write a function that tells Redux how we want state values passed to our component as props. Additionally, we have to tell the component about any actions that it might want to dispatch.

Here is the general pattern that we'll follow when connecting components:

```
connect(
  mapStateToProps,
  mapDispatchToProps
)(Component);
```

Here's a breakdown of how this works:

- The `connect()` function from the React-Redux package returns a new React component.
- The `mapStateToProps()` function takes a state argument and returns an object with property values based on this state.
- The `mapDispatchToProps()` function takes a `dispatch()` argument, which is used to dispatch actions, and returns an object with functions that can dispatch actions. These are added to the component's props.
- `Component` is a React component that you want connected to the Redux store.

As you start connecting components, you'll soon realize that Redux is taking care of many React component lifecycle chores for you. Where you would typically need to implement `componentDidMount()` functionality, suddenly, you don't need to. This leads to clean and concise React components.

Connecting the stream component

Let's take a look at the `Stream` component:

```
import React, { Component } from 'react';
import { connect } from 'react-redux';

import StreamTweet from './StreamTweet';
import Header from './Header';
import TweetStore from '../stores/TweetStore';

class Stream extends Component {
  render() {
    const { tweet } = this.props;
    const { onAddTweetToCollection } = this.props;
    const headerText =
    'Waiting for public photos from Twitter...';

    if (tweet) {
      return (<StreamTweet tweet={tweet}/>);
    }

    return (<Header text={headerText}/>);
  }
}

const mapStateToProps = ({ tweet }) => ({ tweet });

const mapDispatchToProps = dispatch => ({});

export default connect(
  mapStateToProps,
  mapDispatchToProps
)(Stream);
```

Not much about `Stream` has changed from its previous implementation. The main difference is that we've removed some lifecycle methods. All of the Redux connection code comes after the component declaration. The `mapStateToProps()` function returns the `tweet` property from the state. So now our component has a `tweet` prop. The `mapDispatchToProps()` function returns an empty object because `Stream` doesn't dispatch any actions. You don't actually have to provide this function when you have no actions. However, this might change in the future, and if the function is already there, you just need to add properties to the object.

Connecting the StreamTweet component

The `Stream` component renders the `StreamTweet` component, so let's take a look at this next:

```
import React, { Component } from 'react';
import { connect } from 'react-redux';

import ReactDOM from 'react-dom';
import Header from './Header';
import Tweet from './Tweet';
import store from '../stores';
import { addTweetToCollection } from '../actions';

class StreamTweet extends Component {
  render() {
    const { tweet, onImageClick } = this.props;

    return (
      <section>
        <Header text="Latest public photo from Twitter"/>
        <Tweet
          tweet={tweet}
          onImageClick={onImageClick}
        />
      </section>
    );
  }
}

const mapStateToProps = state => ({});

const mapDispatchToProps = (dispatch, ownProps) => ({
  onImageClick: () => {
    dispatch(addTweetToCollection(ownProps.tweet));
  }
});

export default connect(
  mapStateToProps,
  mapDispatchToProps
)(StreamTweet);
```

The `StreamTweet` component doesn't actually use any state from the Redux store. So why bother connecting it? The answer is, so that we can map action dispatcher functions to component props. Remember, action creator functions in Redux apps just return the action object instead of dispatching the action.

In the `mapDispatchToProps()` function here, we're dispatching an `addTweetToCollection()` action by passing its return value to `dispatch()`. Redux provides us with a simple dispatch function that's bound to the Redux store. Any time we want to dispatch an action, we can just call `dispatch()`. Now the `StreamTweet` component will have an `onImageClick()` function prop that can be used as an event handler to handle the click events.

Connecting the collection component

Now we just have to connect the `Collection` component and its child components. Here's what the `Collection` component looks like:

```
import React, { Component } from 'react';
import ReactDOMServer from 'react-dom/server';
import { connect } from 'react-redux';

import CollectionControls from './CollectionControls';
import TweetList from './TweetList';
import Header from './Header';
import CollectionUtils from '../utils/CollectionUtils';

class Collection extends Component {
  createHtmlMarkupStringOfTweetList() {
    const { collectionTweets } = this.props;
    const htmlString = ReactDOMServer.renderToStaticMarkup(
      <TweetList tweets={collectionTweets}/>
    );

    const htmlMarkup = {
      html: htmlString
    };

    return JSON.stringify(htmlMarkup);
  }

  render() {
    const { collectionTweets } = this.props;
```

```
    const numberOfTweetsInCollection = CollectionUtils
      .getNumberOfTweetsInCollection(collectionTweets);
    let htmlMarkup;

    if (numberOfTweetsInCollection > 0) {
      htmlMarkup = this.createHtmlMarkupStringOfTweetList();

      return (
        <div>
          <CollectionControls
            numberOfTweetsInCollection=
            {numberOfTweetsInCollection}
            htmlMarkup={htmlMarkup}
          />

          <TweetList tweets={collectionTweets} />
        </div>
      );
    }

    return (<Header text="Your collection is empty"/>);
  }
}

const mapStateToProps = state => state.collection;

const mapDispatchToProps = dispatch => ({});

export default connect(
  mapStateToProps,
  mapDispatchToProps
)(Collection);
```

The Collection component doesn't dispatch any actions, so our
mapDispatchToProps() function returns an empty object. It does use state from the
Redux store though, so our mapStateToProps() implementation returns state.
collection. This is how we slice the state of the entire application into pieces that
the component cares about. For example, if our component needed access to some
other state in addition to Collection, we'd return a new object made up of different
slices of the overall state.

Connecting collection controls

Within the `Collection` component, we have the `CollectionControls` component. Let's see what it looks like once it's been connected to the Redux store:

```
import React, { Component } from 'react';
import { connect } from 'react-redux';

import Header from './Header';
import Button from './Button';
import CollectionRenameForm from './CollectionRenameForm';
import CollectionExportForm from './CollectionExportForm';
import {
  toggleIsEditingName,
  removeAllTweetsFromCollection
} from '../actions';

class CollectionControls extends Component {
  getHeaderText = () => {
    const { numberOfTweetsInCollection } = this.props;
    const { collectionName } = this.props;
    let text = numberOfTweetsInCollection;

    if (numberOfTweetsInCollection === 1) {
      text = `${text} tweet in your`;
    } else {
      text = `${text} tweets in your`;
    }

    return (
      <span>
        {text} <strong>{collectionName}</strong> collection
      </span>
    );
  }

  render() {
    const {
      collectionName,
      isEditingName,
      htmlMarkup,
      onRenameCollection,
      onEmptyCollection
    } = this.props;
```

```
      if (isEditingName) {
        return (
          <CollectionRenameForm name={collectionName}/>
        );
      }

      return (
        <div>
          <Header text={this.getHeaderText()}/>

          <Button
            label="Rename collection"
            handleClick={onRenameCollection}
          />

          <Button
            label="Empty collection"
            handleClick={onEmptyCollection}
          />

          <CollectionExportForm
            html={htmlMarkup}
            title={collectionName}
          />
        </div>
      );
    }
  }
}

const mapStateToProps = state => state.collection;

const mapDispatchToProps = dispatch => ({
  onRenameCollection: () => {
    dispatch(toggleIsEditingName());
  },
  onEmptyCollection: () => {
    dispatch(removeAllTweetsFromCollection());
  }
});

export default connect(
  mapStateToProps,
  mapDispatchToProps
)(CollectionControls);
```

This time, we have a component that requires objects from both `mapStateToProps()` and `mapDispatchToProps()`. Once again, we need to pass the collection state to this component as props. The `onRenameCollection()` event handler dispatches a `toggleIsEditingName()` action while the `onEmptyCollection()` event handler dispatches the `removeAllTweetsFromCollection()` action.

Connecting the TweetList component

Lastly, we have the `TweetList` component; let's take a look:

```
import React, { Component } from 'react';
import { connect } from 'react-redux';

import Tweet from './Tweet';
import { removeTweetFromCollection } from '../actions';

const listStyle = {
  padding: '0'
};

const listItemStyle = {
  display: 'inline-block',
  listStyle: 'none'
};

class TweetList extends Component {
  getListOfTweetIds = () =>
    Object.keys(this.props.tweets);

  getTweetElement = (tweetId) => {
    const {
      tweets,
      onRemoveTweetFromCollection
    } = this.props;
    const tweet = tweets[tweetId];

    return (
      <li style={listItemStyle} key={tweet.id}>
        <Tweet
          tweet={tweet}
          onImageClick={onRemoveTweetFromCollection}
        />
      </li>
    );
```

```
    }

    render() {
      const tweetElements = this
        .getListOfTweetIds()
        .map(this.getTweetElement);

      return (
        <ul style={listStyle}>
          {tweetElements}
        </ul>
      );
    }
  }

  const mapStateToProps = () => ({});

  const mapDispatchToProps = dispatch => ({
    onRemoveTweetFromCollection: ({ id }) => {
      dispatch(removeTweetFromCollection(id));
    }
  });

  export default connect(
    mapStateToProps,
    mapDispatchToProps
  )(TweetList);
```

This component doesn't depend on the Redux store for any state. It does map an action dispatcher function to its props though. We don't necessarily need to connect the dispatcher here. For example, if this component's parent is connecting functions to the dispatcher, the function could be declared there and passed into this component as a prop. The benefit would be that `TweetList` would no longer require Redux at all. The downside would be having too many dispatch functions declared in one component. Luckily, you get to implement your component using whichever approach you see fit.

Creating stores and wiring your app

We're almost done refactoring our Snapterest app from a traditional Flux architecture, to one that's based on Redux. There's just two things left to do.

First, we have to combine our reducer functions into a single function in order to make a store:

```
import { combineReducers } from 'redux'
import collection from './collection';
import tweet from './tweet';

const reducers = combineReducers({
  collection,
  tweet
})

export default reducers;
```

This uses the `combineReducers()` function to take our two existing reducer functions that exist in their own modules, and produces a single reducer that we can use to make a Redux store:

```
import { createStore } from 'redux';
import reducers from '../reducers';

export default createStore(reducers);
```

There you have it—our Redux store is created, complete with its initial state that's supplied by reducer functions by default. Now we just have to pass this store to our top-level React component:

```
import React from 'react';
import ReactDOM from 'react-dom';
import { Provider } from 'react-redux';

import Application from './components/Application';
import { initializeStreamOfTweets } from './utils/WebAPIUtils';
import store from './stores';

initializeStreamOfTweets(store);

ReactDOM.render(
  <Provider store={store}>
    <Application/>
  </Provider>,
  document.getElementById('react-application')
);
```

The `Provider` component wraps our top-level application component and provides it, along with any child components that depend on an application state, with state updates.

Summary

In this chapter, you learned how to refine your Flux architecture using the Redux library. Redux applications should have only one store, action creators can be simple, and reducer functions control the transformation of the immutable state. The aim of Redux, in a nutshell, is to reduce the number of moving parts typically found in a traditional Flux architecture while retaining the unidirectional dataflow.

You then implemented the Snapterest application using Redux. Starting with the reducers, you returned a new state for the Redux store any time a valid action was dispatched. Then you built action creator functions that returned an object with the correct type property. Lastly, you refactored components so that they were connected to Redux. You made sure that the components could read store data as well as dispatch actions.

This is a wrap for this book. I hope you've learned enough about the essentials of React development that you can continue your journey of discovery by learning more advanced React topics. More importantly, I hope you learned more about React by building awesome React apps and then making them better.

Index

Symbols

A

action creator
creating 158, 159
Application component
refactoring 182-184
asynchronous rendering 4

B

Babel
URL 23, 41
Bootstrap
URL 65
building 19
build process 20
Button component
creating 123, 124

C

camelCase naming convention 52
children parameter 33-38
CodePen
URL 61, 125
CollectionActionCreators
creating 180, 181
Collection component
creating 97-102
refactoring 184-187
CollectionControls component
creating 110-116
refactoring 187, 189

CollectionExportForm component
creating 125
collection reducers
about 197, 198
names, editing 200
name, setting 200
tweets, adding 198, 199
tweets, removing 199
CollectionRenameForm component
creating 117-123
refactoring 189-192
CollectionStore
creating 175-180
component lifecycle
about 76
componentDidUpdate method 90
componentWillReceiveProps method 86-88
componentWillUpdate method 89, 90
methods 76
shouldComponentUpdate method 89
updating methods 85, 86
components
action creators, mapping to props 203
app, wiring 211, 212
collection component, connecting 206, 207
collection controls, connecting 208, 210
connecting, to application state 203
error handling 5
state, mapping to props 203
stores, creating 211, 212
stream component, connecting 204
StreamTweet component,
connecting 205, 206
TweetList component, connecting 210, 211
container React component
creating 61-69

Content Security Policies (CSP)
URL 92

D

dispatcher
  creating 158
Document Object Model (DOM) 28
Don't Repeat Yourself (DRY) 18

E

elements
  rendering 6
Enzyme 144
error boundary 5
expectations
  creating 128-139

F

failing test 132
fiber 4
Flux
  about 156, 157
  concerns, decoupling 166-168
  exploring 194
  URL 194

G

getters methods 171
Git
  installing 13
  URL 13

J

Jasmine 128
JavaScript
  used, for creating React elements 30-32
JavaScript DOM API
  references 28
JavaScript run-to-completion thread 4
Jest
  about 128
  executing 133
  installing 132, 133
  URL 132

Jest command-line interface (Jest CLI) 132
JSX
  used, for creating elements 39-41

K

Key-Value Observation (KVO) 29

M

matcher function 132
mock 128
mocking 128
modular 19
modules 19
mounting methods
  about 78
  componentDidMount method 80-82
  componentWillMount method 78, 80
multiple tests
  creating 134-139

N

Node.js
  about 12
  installing 12
  references 12
Node.js modules
  reusing 19, 20
npm
  about 18
  installing 12
  reference 12

P

package 18
package.json
  creating 18
  URL 18
packaging 19
Pinterest
  URL 11
portals
  rendering 7
project
  approaching 11

project structure
  creating 17
props parameter 32

R

React
  children parameter 33-38
  elements, creating with JavaScript 30, 32
  elements, creating with JSX 39, 41
  elements, rendering 38, 39
  installing 30
  props parameter 32
  references 10
  type parameter 32
  URL 30, 41
  used, for problem solving 57-59
React application
  planning 59-61
React component properties
  setting 91-94
  validating 94-96
React components
  library, using 71-75
  testing 140-151
React component's lifecycle methods
  about 76-78
  mounting 76, 78
  unmounting 76, 82
  updating 76
reducers
  about 196, 197
  collection reducers 197
  tweet reducers 201
  used, for controlling state 196
Redux
  Flux, using 196
  one store 195, 196
  parts, moving 196
  state, controlling with reducers 196
  using 195

S

Search Engine Optimization (SEO) 39
setter methods 171
single direction 156
Single Page Application (SPA) 27

Snapkite Engine
  about 14, 71
  URL 15
  used, for data filtering 14-16
Snapkite Filter
  references 15
snapshot testing 148
Snapterest 11 57
source-to-source compilation 23
specs
  creating 128-131
state
  controlling, with reducers 196
stateful React component
  creating 50-55
stateless React component
  about 44
  creating 44-49
  versus stateful React component 43
store
  creating 159-163
Stream component
  refactoring 169-174
StreamTweet component
  refactoring 193
strings
  rendering 6

T

test() function
  test implementation 130
  test name 130
test suits
  creating 128-132
this.props 50
this.state 50
transpilation 23
TweetList component
  creating 105-109
  onRemoveTweetFromCollection
      property 102
  refactoring 192
  tweets property 102
tweet reducers
  about 201
  simplified action creators 201, 202

tweets, receiving 201
Twitter
  references 13
Twitter Streaming API
  data, obtaining 13
  references 14
type parameter 32

U

unit tests
  writing 127
unmounting methods
  about 82
  componentWillUnmount method 83
user interface (UI) 28

V

virtual DOM 29

W

web application
  architecture, analyzing 154, 155
Webpack
  URL 19, 21
  used, for building projects 20-24
web page
  creating 25

www.ingramcontent.com/pod-product-compliance
Lightning Source LLC
LaVergne TN
LVHW081522050326
832903LV00025B/1591